A Passion for Seeing

SRI LANKA

A Passion for Seeing

ON BEING AN IMAGE MAKER

FREDERICK FRANCK

An Anthology of
Writings, Drawings and Sculptures
1959-2003

Foreword by David Appelbaum
Design by Martin Moskof

NEW PALTZ · NEW YORK

Library of Congress Cataloging-in-Publication Data

Franck, Frederick, 1909-

A passion for seeing: confessions of a driven image-maker / Frederick Franck

p. cm.

ISBN 1-930337-06-X (pb.: alk. paper)

1. Spiritual life. 2. Franck, Frederick, 1909- I. Title.

BL624 .F7196 2002

709'.2--dc21

Table of Contents

Dedicated
In warm friendship
to
Ann Roberts

Foreword

Like his beloved Angelus Silenus, Frederick Franck is adept in depicting the expressions of our Original Face. His life-work is compendious. Its vast extent explores both the height to which humanity eternally aspires and the depths to which it repeatedly sinks. In vivid images of war—in stone, metal, wood, ink, and words—he reminds us of the apocalypse that looms should we fail in our aspirations. On the many ceramic faces of a sculpture entitled Incarnatons of the Humanum, we catch spectral reflections of the nuclear blast that leveled Nagasaki. Beholding the likenesses of God within those startled countenances, we can avow with renewed conviction, "Never again." Frederick Franck's work is a perpetual prayer for peace.

He implores us not only visually but also through thought. Above all, he asks that we recall the meaning of life, which, in the words of Hui Neng, Sixth Zen Patriarch, is to see. What is seeing but a pathway to divine knowledge? It leads through the valley of the shadow of death—the inferno—through purgatory, and end with paradise and love, and is portrayed in all its rich, sober humor. We ascend in and through a silence that empties us of attachments and liberates the soul to a life of service. The restorative power of an undying hope supports the effort. This we learn most poignantly from the figure of the prophet Ezekiel, who is central to Franck's revelation. Ezekiel had a heart of stone until God replaced it with one of flesh. In his renewal, he came to understand the life beyond life—and the Absolute Other—and could embrace wholeness. For

Frederick Franck, Ezekiel's hope is humanity's. He would have us expand our horizons until, empty of all things, we can see with the eye that, Meister Eckhart says, sees the same thing as God sees.

He uses the word trans-religious to describe his unique approach, best seen in person by a walk through his marvelous museum and sculpture garden of Pacem in Terris, located by his home and work place. Through a creative synthesis, Frederick Franck revitalizes idea, image and symbol drawn from Eastern and Western traditions. They inscribe his work with a force, universally recognized as spirit. Spirit is what humanity presently lacks, but needs in order to elevate its sight. The stations of the cross as well as the classic Zen oxherding series picture the suffering by which the eye is raised toward the Lord within. Spirit so portrayed lets us dwell where we are, between earth and heaven, heaven and earth. It lets us receive the gift of silence that moves the intelligence to the supreme beauty of all things. Awareness of that, Frederick Franck tells us, is what we most seek— being human against all odds. The extent to which we are recalled to that awareness by his many texts and drawings in this special anthology, to that extent we will be able to take a step back from the probable ruin of the abyss. In the repose of the earth, wherein Frederick Franck's art work keeps a silent vigil, we find a way again to lie beside the still waters.

— *David Appelbaum*

Prelude

I was born in 1909, the fateful year Louis Bleriot became the first non-bird ever to fly across the Channel. Nobody realized that this feat would mark the birth of a brand new era in which humans would fly across the Atlantic for a business lunch in London, and across the Pacific for a symposium in Bombay, or to flatten cities in Japan and Twin Towers in New York.

On August 4, 1914, I was awakened by the opening salvos of the 20th century starting in earnest. The Kaiser's armies had invaded Belgium, half a mile from our doorstep. The German field guns booming just across the border, set our house a-tremble. From my attic window, in horror, I watched the little city of Visay burning under a scarlet sky.

Almost at once the endless files of wretched people fleeing their burning villages, wounded and dying soldiers on pushcarts and trucks, were crossing the border into Holland, which managed to remain neutral in this First World War.

Looking down from our second floor window, I saw people carrying children and belongings on their backs. I still see—eighty eight years later as if it were this morning—the old man carrying his canary in a cage. He looked up at me. I stood there crying, a little bunch of grapes in my hand and threw a few of my grapes to him, in a gesture of desperate compassion. And so from my fifth to my ninth year I was peering into hell from our neutral grand-

stand, sickened by that incurable, life-long allergy to war, to all physical violence.

It was in second grade that I spotted the little German bi-plane above our schoolyard, saw the pilot look down from his open cockpit, all leather cap and goggles who,

violating our neutral airspace, dropped his bomb. It landed close to where I stood, but failed to explode.

Thanks to a sequence of such merciful malfunctions I outlived almost the full length of the century, surviving its continuum of mass murder, and even Franco, Hitler, Stalin, Mao, and their ghoulish ilk, who massacred millions in this beastly century that was—almost inconceivably—also that of Gandhi, Albert Schweitzer, Martin Luther King, Pope John XXIII, among many lesser-known incarnations of humanness, who answered the question what it means to be human with their very lives, that primal question to which all other ones, whether political, economic, religious, artistic, are secondary at best.

Four years later, on November 11, 1918, the Armistice was signed, the nightmare seemed to be over, Germany was defeated.

I remember standing on the railroad platform of Maastricht watching a train consisting of a huge locomotive and a single carriage slowly pass by. It must have stopped for a moment, for I saw an angry old face, Kaiser Wilhelm's, looking out of the carriage window, still in his gold-braided uniform, his turned-up waxed mustache in his haughty face, staring at

me—or so I remember it—and behind him his tall son, the Crown Prince, who would also be interned in the Netherlands on the little island of Wieringen in the Zuiderzee. Wilhelm himself was lodged in the small castle of Doorn, where he amused himself cutting down young trees with a hatchet—and then he died, there or somewhere else.

Defeated Germany was in total chaos. The German mark was devalued to the point where a loaf of pumpernickel cost well over a million marks.

Dutch housewives, moved by the hunger of children in Germany and Austria started organizations offering temporary hospitality to these hungry children. My parents too decided to feed one of them.

I still see Hermann standing on our doorstep, a pale kid, a little rucksack on his back. He was as thin as an asparagus, with a yellowish, long face from which watery blue eyes glared at me, frightened and frightening. His family name was strange, perhaps Polish, I never forgot it: Hermann Pohorille. He was a bit older than I, about twelve. He hardly spoke, but ate like a wolf. He did not play with me. His passion was to catch flies. When he caught one, he would at once pull out its wings, grimacing triumphantly. I begged him to stop. But he just would catch the next one and add it to the heap on the kitchen table, some still crawling. I became so despondent by Hermann's sport that my mother had to find another hostess for him.

He must have been in his early thirties when Hitler came to power and I imagined him in a greenish

grey uniform with swastikas on the collar in Mauthausen or Birkenau, pulling out the wings of humans officially demoted by the Nazis to the status of vermin.

I was half awake this morning when again I saw that train crawl by, saw the Kaiser's wrathful look, and how, suddenly, the train took a little jump as carriages were added, then gained speed so fast that Wilhelm could barely grab a curtain to avoid keeling over. I saw his carriage disappear into the black tunnel at the end of the platform where two men in frock coats lifted their top hats, and a corpulent nun in white habit stood rigidly at attention.

Only then I realized that the train had become longer and longer, thundering past, disappearing into the tunnel.

I stood there, waiting for it to end, but it never ended... it never ended...

A Passion for Seeing

CHAPTER I

❖

1989

❖

FROM

*Life
Drawing
Life*

Published by
GREAT OCEAN PUBLISHING

One of my childhood idols was a local artist, an emaciated fellow, that "fool," who in his threadbare much too large overcoat, stood fervently scribbling down the kids on the merry-go-round. The day I saw him standing with his note pad in the middle of a muddy field, ecstatically trying to catch a flight of starlings with his pencil, his thin colorless whiskers blowing in the wind, he filled me with such reverence that I never dared to talk to him. Moreover he was quite old, perhaps even over forty. But nevertheless I felt not only akin to him, but saw him as by far the most lovable human being around.

The other day, listening to a Bach concerto, I saw him standing there in that field, as if it were today and suddenly remembered his name, Mr. Bachhoven: cruel pun on Bach/Beethoven? On the contrary, I was deeply moved.

•

I too was a loner, an inveterate hiker. I rambled through the hills on our peaceful side of the Border, drank in the glory of white clouds over a meadow full of yellow buttercups, a wayside cross at dusk. But there was always the unbearable accompaniment of this bliss by inescapable terror, the overwhelming confrontation with frightful suffering, one's impotent compassion.

•

Hokusai wrote:

"At seventy-three I learned a little about the real structure of animals, plants, birds, fishes and insects. Consequently when I am eighty I'll have made more progress. At ninety I'll have penetrated the mystery of things. At a hundred I shall have reached something marvelous, but when I am a hundred and ten everything I do, the smallest dot, will be alive."

•

Seeing/drawing a face I sometimes feel it is the human karma I am drawing. Not only that of the person in front of me, but all who went before from the beginningless beginning. It is as if through this one face the entire past and present of our species discloses itself: its "Original Face," as Zen calls it, its Specific Humanness.

The death mask—whether that of Napoleon, Beethoven or that famous one of an unknown girl drowned in the Seine river, reveals the Original Face, its Specific Humanness, freed from all conditioning, unlabeled and timeless.

"In all faces is seen the Face of faces, veiled as in a riddle," says Nicholas of Cusa (14th C.) And a Japanese senryu says:

At last
with his dead face
he looks human

CHAPTER II

1979

FROM

The Awakened Eye

Published by
ALFRED A. KNOPF/VINTAGE

When I was a little boy my grandfather's house was full of treasures. Grandfather had an enormous roll-top desk of shiny mahogany that matched his bookcases with their beveled glass doors. In those bookcases stood all the classics in gold-embossed leather bindings, and an encyclopedia in which I diligently studied the fold-out "Human Anatomy-Female," until Anna, his housekeeper with her glassy—or perhaps glass—left eye and improbably high bosom, would slam it shut and snatch it away.

The greatest treasure of all, however, was the one Grandfather referred to as his "stereopticon." To this "stereopticon" I probably owe my way of life. The antique gadget consisted of twin lenses in a leather-covered housing, lined with red velvet. From this housing a kind of slide rule jutted forward, with a device at its end in which you placed twin photographs. Then, pressing the velvet edge to your face, you saw through the lenses an oak, not flat as in a picture, but all in the round, as a living presence. For hours I could sit and watch the miraculous, living three-dimensionality of cows in a meadow, lovers kissing under a lilac bush, Queen Wilhelmina of the Netherlands on her black steed, rotund ladies of Toulouse Lautrec in stays and garter belts…

And so it came about that sometimes, when getting tired on the long, lonely hikes I loved—the fields, hills and hedges began to look listless and flat in a dull two-dimensionality, I found I could order my eyes: "Now look through the stereopticon!" They would obey and the third dimension was at once restored.

Every sprig of grass came to life and stood there separately in its own space; clumps of trees broke up into individual beings, each one springing from its own roots, deep in the earth. People, when looked at through my mental stereopticon, underwent an extraordinary metamorphosis: each one became the impressively unique, mysterious being he never expected himself to be, that which, when merely looked at, was mailman, poplar or squirrel became—when seen stereoptically—unnamable, ineffable.

I found my trick of stereoscopic seeing such a precious secret that I never mentioned it to anyone until now. But I practiced it as often as I could, and discovered that seeing things and beings stereoptically could take the place of a lot of thinking "about" them.

I now realize that Grandfather's stereopticon was the mute Master who initiated me into seeing, gave me the first hint of the potentiality of my everyday eye to become an awakened eye, an eye that can do more than merely look at things in order to recognize them, an eye that can really see the Ten Thousand Things, not just-as-they-are, but such-as-they-are: in their meaning, their truth and totality. It gave me a first taste of contemplation.

When all looks dull and déjà-vu, I can still command my eye to see stereoptically, and make it awaken from its routine slumber...

While seeing/drawing a beech tree, a leaf, a face, I see it "through the stereopticon" in three dimensions. But recently a fourth dimension has been added. Not only do I see it in space, I see it in time: in its time. The form of a tree is its time: seen in space, its pattern is that of its growing, its being, its time...The face I draw changes its feature play constantly. The leaf I just picked is already going limp, then I see it shrivel. While seeing/drawing I see each thing living its own time, as I am living my time, my life-time. The awakened eye becomes utterly aware of the fleetingness of all that passes before it, of this eye still seeing, of this hand still moving, still tracing...

The ego has become harmless to other beings, it has lost its sting, it has "turned around at its base," has come to see itself to be: *neither I nor other, both I and other.*

Enlightenment may simply be sanity! The Sanity in which I see my real situation in the living fabric of all that exists. It is the ultimate Sanity that has also been called sanctity.

Joshu's tree stands in my own front yard, as it stood in the park where, as a boy, I embraced and kissed it—stealthily, when no one was looking...I saw my neighbor cut down Joshu's tree, just to try out his new power saw. He was proud of it as he is proud of having shot a little rabbit, or even an old carp near our waterfall, for he does not know, as Chuang Tzu knew, "the joy of fishes, as I walk along the river." Nor does he see, as Wenshi saw:

Just pick up anything you like:
in everything It is so nakedly manifested...

I used to love drawing France more than Italy, Holland more than either, and all of these

LIEGE

more than America. This was long ago, and I don't know how it happened, but no longer partial, my eyes now love the spot my feet happen to stand on.

•

Sometimes when women—especially fashionable ladies—look at my drawings "from life" they wonder aloud: "But why do you have to draw such awful (or old, or flabby, or scrawny) women?" I detect an element of fear in such questions.

I am so much less fascinated by standardized prettiness than by the infinite variations on the human theme! The fat, the skinny, the flabby and the old are not awful! That which life has marked, wounded, does not repel but moves me.

I could draw it every day if it were not in such short supply, hiding itself in shame, to honor and cherish that which is neither contemptible, trivial nor frivolous: the human, the Real.

Yes, seeing/drawing is the "subversive activity" that runs counter to all the rules of the art game. Its "originality" consists in the return to your own origin: it is authentic, free from borrowed isms.

•

I fly home to Warwick, and find myself walking a quarter-mile along the country road behind our house. The hills and hedges and fences are celebrating the rites of spring. Grasses and vines and meadow flowers are dancing in the wind. The fresh viridian of cornfields sway in gentle waves. A huge swarm of sparrows tumbles out of cloudless blue, a red-winged blackbird sits on top of the hedge whistling the Dharma.

Grasses and weeds, apple blossoms and rocks, you and I grow out of Earth as the hairs grow out of our skins. Skunk cabbage, field mouse and fly reveal stupefying marvels, loom up from Emptiness, arise and disappear in It.

"The material thing before you, that is it," says Huang Po. Yes. But to the unawakened eye that does not see but looks "It" is just material things…The eye that merely looks-at is a not-yet-quite human eye.

The unawakened eye is closer to that of hawk or rat, apprehends only prey and enemy, a pre-human eye in a human skull, limited to recognizing and appraising in direct relation to its cravings and its fears. The fully human eye is this same eye, once it is awakened.

Astonishingly, the contemporary eye, blunted by a constant stream of photographic and electronic glamour and horror, when confronted with live reality has not yet lost all compassion and sensitiveness. It seems to be protected by an imperishable grace, for it is still capable of being awakened, of Seeing the supreme miracle, that of sheer Existence . . . .

•

I was five years old. My mother and a friend I was expected to address as "Aunt" had taken us children to a modest little tea garden with swings and seesaws on the edge of our small town on the Dutch-Belgian border. It sported the elegant French name of "Les Champs Elysées": the Elysian Fields—the Celestial Fields of Bliss…I can still see and hear the trio that was playing on the rickety bandstand: the thin, sorrowful violinist in his patent leather shoes, the bald, rotund pianist, the bosomy lady in white tulle, a moaning cello clamped between her short, plump thighs. The other children were still swinging and seesawing when I got bored, as mother and the pseudo-aunt with her long nose were absorbed in the music—which did not prevent them from chattering rapturously in whispers—I saw my chance to escape across a narrow stream, and found myself in a sun-drenched meadow. I lay down in the fragrant, swaying grass, tall enough to make me unfindable, and listened to the trio far away. Then, suddenly, there was a loud zooming close to my ear and I was terrified: a velvety bee circled around my head, almost touching it. But ignoring me, it sat down on a hairy purple flower that was so close to my head that it looked huge and vague, and started to suck…At that moment something happened: all my fear evaporated, but so did bee and sun and grass…and I. For at that instant sunlight and sky, grasses, bee and I merged, fused, became one—yet remained sun and sky and grass and bee and I. It lasted for a heartbeat, an hour, a year…Then, as abruptly, I was I again, but filled with an indescribable bliss—were they not Elysian Fields?

The trio was still playing the tune that I remember to this day, and I can whistle it for you anytime you wish…I had probably come as close to Reality as I ever was to come in this life.

In the silence of drawing
hidden, yet visible, in each face
I see the "Face of faces,"
see:
that the plural of man
does not exist,
is our cruelest hallucination—
see that our Oneness is infinite differentiation,
see:

that the pattern of the universe
and mine
are not-two,
that what lives in me
is the Tao
in which all lives.
This is not what I believe
but what my eyes
saw on the way.

Having become
all these faces, all these bodies,
a meadow, a flower,
a night moth and a cow,
a stranger no longer
I am at home,
beloved earth!

The Hwa Yen Sutra says:
"The incalculable eons are but one moment—
and this moment is no moment."

The 7th-century masters had become aware of time as composed of ultra-short time—fragments which they called NEN, thought-moments of such flashing brevity that for all practical purposes they could be called timeless. The NEN theory is not easy to follow, but once grasped I found it as illuminating as it is provocative.

When my eye perceives something in the outer world, it registers it during the first, immeasurably short micro-instant or NEN, in a direct vision which is purely intuitive and cognitive, as in a flash of profound insight into that which is seen. This first micro-instant of direct apprehension or in-sight into Reality, however, is followed immediately by a "second NEN," and with the same lightning speed by a "third NEN." The "second NEN" is a flash of mental reflection, of becoming aware of my intuitive insight, of this profound "knowing." But in the "third NEN," which follows just as rapidly, this awareness becomes "my" awareness: both previous flashes become integrated in my continuous stream of consciousness; are processed, as it were, in that region of the mind where reasoning, labeling, introspection—in short, my ego annexes everything. The experience now becomes part of "my" consciousness and at once the Me begins to interpret, to rationalize and to draw "logical" conclusions from the direct perception, to distort the direct, "clairvoyant" grasp of the first NEN, and to imprison it once more in words and concepts. These cogitations, analyses and conclusions snowball further until the intuitive revelation of the first NEN is totally lost.

Another way in which the ancients handled their momentous discovery was to speak of a "first-NEN ego" which is capable of that pure intuitive knowledge beyond thinking of which Christ's words from the apocryphal Gospel of St. Thomas seem to speak: "You cannot take hold of it, yet you cannot lose it." They called "second-NEN ego" the awareness of this direct perception, while the "third-NEN ego" synthesizes both first- and second-NEN egos into that empirical ego, the "little self" we speak of as "Me." The "Me" is no longer identified with what this eye perceived, but has already "objectified" it, that is: it has made it into an object, a thing…nothing is left of the first-NEN vision

except its distortion. "Me" (which itself is the I-feeling-objectified) and "It" are now at opposite poles. For the "Me" imagines itself to be the center of the world, and in its delusion takes itself to be the only really valid observer of the outside world, as a permanent and autonomous entity that is more real than anything else.

A senryu says:
All the people I meet
make faces
as if they were going to live
forever.

What does all this have to do with seeing/drawing or with drawing in line instead of in blotches?…

Everything!! The discipline of seeing/drawing is that of becoming all eye: that is, of seeing with the first NEN, so that each touch, each impact of pen on paper jumps from retina to hand—short-circuiting the interpretive machinery of the brain's third NEN activity, to land precisely in the right spot. In rapid but quiet succession, uninterrupted by thinking, these first-NEN transcriptions fall into place! My line is the movement from first NEN to first NEN. Or rather: these first NENS precipitate themselves in strokes and dots, and these strokes and dots form a perfectly continuous mosaic of first-NEN imprints which, together, become an image!

The very moment the third NEN (that is: "ME"!) is given the slightest chance to interfere, it takes over and the mosaic is disturbed: all proportions are off, the jigsaw puzzle no longer fits together…Either my lines become a meaningless tangle or I try tricks. I quickly shift to devices, to sleight-of-hand. I switch, for instance, from seeing/drawing to "stylization" or to "shading," or I tell myself I am "creating a design," a "composition," an "abstraction"…Or I succumb to the temptation to start "sketching." Whatever life-buoy I choose, I am no longer one with what I see. I am lost, caught up in conceptualizations.

As far as first NEN is concerned, animals have first-NEN perception only, do not become aware of it in a second NEN, and even less do they integrate these perceptions into a third-NEN ego. My cat is watching a mouse. It transforms her totally in every fiber of her musculature. An almost imperceptible shiver runs through her skin, the sweeping tail lies motionless, the ears stand erect, her face now is an "I see mouse" face…She pounces and "has" the unfortunate mouse.

My own immediate response, my first-NEN perception, is as specifically human as that of my cat is feline. When the mouse's image falls onto my retina, the reflex it releases does not make me pounce. It makes, for instance, my hand trace a line.

Even before the image is labeled "mouse," before the interpreting brain has processed and classified it, it travels through the psychosomatic unit I usually call Me, "through this human heart," to the hand that notes it down. "Absolute seeing" is this seeing in the first NEN, that takes place in the timeless instant in which we humans may intuit the Suchness of what the eye perceives.

CHAPTER III

1965

FROM

Outsider in the Vatican

Published by
MACMILLAN

In the dank, hollow Casa della Missione, Giuseppe Descuffi, Archbishop of Smyrna and Izmir, was waiting for me on the third floor. At the top of the dismal stone staircase, I turned to the right through long corridors that smelled acrid, like a hospital no longer in use. There was a wait after my knock. A very old patriarchal man with a square white beard, thin as a wraith, opened the door. He limped slowly and painfully, "I broke my hip a few months ago," he explained. "I am most flattered that you think me worthy of being sketched," he went on, offering me a chair which he insisted on pulling with great effort closer to the table that served as his desk. "Are you sure you are comfortable there? I am sorry our furniture is not more luxurious."

The long, dark room was cheerless and quite empty. On a floor of waxed planks stood the narrow bed with a banal St. Sulpice crucifix over it; there was the one straight plush armchair with clangy springs on which I was sitting. The wardrobe door stood ajar as if it could not close properly. On the table near the window a chaos of books, pamphlets, and papers. The Latin proceedings of the Council lay open.

"What do you prefer me to do?" the old man asked with exquisite politeness of tone and gesture. He spoke a very elegant French. He actually looked like an ancient impoverished French duke, mid-nineteenth century, elected a member of the French Academy in some recognition of a distinguished work in history or entomology. But he told me he was an Italian, born in Turkey seventy some years ago.

"I don't want to disturb Your Excellency at all," I said in what was to become my stock phrase with the prelates. "Please continue whatever you were doing." The old man coughed a long, hoarse cough.

"I hope it is not too cold for you in this room," he murmured. "I'll go on, then, preparing my statement to the Council for tomorrow." His eyes were very deep-set. He had taken up his pen again and prepared himself to continue writing his statement. To warm up I started to scribble a first sketch. There was a knock. "Oh, how unfortunate that I have to interrupt you," the old archbishop apologized. He limped to the door, gesturing that I should remain seated. A little, plump peasant girl loaded with shirts and clean sheets came in. He bowed to her as though she were a princess. "Just put it on the bed, my dear," he said, holding the door to show her out again. *"Merci infiniment, ma chère fille."* He bowed, closing the door behind her.

•

My appointment to draw Archbishop Van Lierde was for 6:15 PM. That evening I entered the Portone di Bronzo in my black coat, my black suit, carrying the large black drawing portfolio. The Swiss guard knew me by now. "Just go ahead," he gestured.

"How do I find Monsignor van Lierde?" I asked. "Go up the *Scala Regia,* turn right. There is a bell in the *Scala Ducale* with his name on it. Then go up the little staircase on your left." I started to walk up the huge stone stairway. It seemed endless and I got out of breath. Bearers had carried popes innumerable times up and down this Royal Staircase, but I had to walk and drag my portfolio; there was less and less light. Where I had to turn right, the stairs became completely dark. There was not a soul around. At the top I pushed aside the heavy velvet curtain and entered the huge hall, where a tiny bulb was glowing. There were six great ornamental doors. I

tried the first one on my left. It was locked. I tried the second one. It had no nameplate. On my right I moved the leaden velvet curtain away; the door behind it was not locked and as I pushed I found myself in a dark lavatory.

Another door gave way and I stood in a chapel where a priest was in silent prayer. I turned around and tiptoed out. The fourth door had something like a bellpull hanging next to it. I pulled it timidly a few times. No reply. Then I gave it a very energetic pull; the heavy curtain came shut and hit me in the face. The next door opened and I found myself in fresh air in a dimly lit courtyard. The taillight of a big car was visible. "Hello," I cried, "could you tell me—" At that moment the car pulled away. I looked at my watch. It was close to a quarter to seven. My shout had warned someone and a window opened. "I can't find Archbishop van Lierde's bell," I cried out, nearly weeping with rage. "It is in the *Sala Ducale,* first door on your left," a voice answered pleasantly. "I know, but I can't find it!" A young priest came downstairs, crossed the courtyard, and took me to the Archbishop's door. It really existed; this was no Kafka dream. The hall I had been in was the one next to the *Sala Ducale!*

The priest who opened the door told me to wait a few minutes in the dingy little hallway. Two Roman archbishop hats with green tassels were hanging on a hook above heaps of books and officially stamped papers. I was relieved and euphoric now; as I was trying on one of the hats I heard the creaking of a door. I just had time to put on my official face: "Your Exellency, forgive me, I am late. I lost my way." He was about fifty, tall and fleshy, a face gone heavy in which the boy was still visible. He spoke Dutch with precision, but with a Flemish accent that seemed to make it deliberately quaint and archaic. He was very polite, but it was a cold politeness. Had he caught me in his hat, after all? I had the impression he was afraid to seem too informally friendly. We first sat down on little gilt chairs in his anteroom. I had felt that here I had to bring a present, a copy of my *Days with Albert Schweitzer.* He looked at the book and into it. "Is it medical?" he asked after a few moments. "No," I said, "not at all, but I worked on the medical staff of Dr. Schweitzer and I thought this might interest you. It also shows you some of my drawings." "Aha," he said, looking at the book with an uncomprehending stare. "Who is this Dr. Schweitzer, anyhow?" he asked a little suspiciously. "*The* Dr. Schweitzer, Your Excellency." Had he never really heard of him? I told him about my work in Lambarene and then about Schweitzer's Nobel Prize. "Aha," he said again, "Of course, of course. Indeed."

"Where do you want to draw me?" he asked. "Here, or behind my desk?" "Maybe behind your desk. I would prefer you to work or read as usual." He went before me into his study and started to clear his desk. "Not necessary, Your Excellency, not at all. I leave all that out anyway." "Oh, no, dear sir, I can't stand this disorder while you are drawing me." "I just want you to be yourself, Your Excellency, and read or work." "I'll say my prayers if you don't mind," he said a little sharply. "Of course, Your Excellency, as you wish." "Well, you see, I have to. I am not through for the day. Are you comfortable in that chair?" "Yes, indeed, I am, thank you," I said, wiping away the first drops of sweat. "Are you sure? I can give you another chair. With pleasure."

The prayer book was lying in front of him. He pulled a precious ornamental crucifix closer and folded his hands, fixing the ring so that its fine stone reflected the light from the desk lamp. I had started my warming-up scribble. "I am so sorry, but I really must pray," he started again in his very formal English. "There are certain prayers which—Can you see me well this way?" "Excellent," I said, "perfect." "Or rather this way," he went on, as if he had not heard me, keeping his hands folded but turning his face a little toward me, and then away again, eyeing the ceiling. I did not reply, but scribbled a second sketch. What was getting on my paper looked horrifying. Fingers can be tongue-tied too. The sweat was dripping. "You are sure this is the right angle," His Excellency asked, looking up from his prayer book, "and that you are perfectly comfortable? Make yourself completely at home, dear sir." "Of course, Your Excellency." I tore off a new sheet and started again. I too was praying now.

"I'll finish my prayers quite soon, then I can do something else," the Archbishop said reassuringly. "Oh, no," I said, and though I could not imagine my expression I did not like my tone of voice, "there is nothing more inspiring to draw than a man in communication with his God." The Bishop kept his pose this time, but he turned his eyes toward me under his long eyelids and gave me a strange, poisonous look. "May I see what you have been doing?" he asked when at last I gave up.

"Oh," I said, using one of those unblinking lies I have practiced to perfection, "these are only notes I take on the spot. At home I work them out and make a synthesis." This lets me off the hook of criticism.

Back in New York I carefully chose the two sketches in which he looked almost human, had them photostated, and sent them off. The Bishop thanked me in English; he wrote:

"Will you allow me just to express a judgment? It is that I think both pictures good, and true. Only, the underlip, and the part of the face under the lips, is not pleasing as it is. I find that the expression has the effect of being somewhat moody, unsatisfied, tired, or lacking in serenity—I mean only from this part of the face as it results. If you could take this out I should be happy and pleased. This is my humble opinion, as regards an effect which strikes me in your beautiful work. With my sincere gratitude and admiration…"

My next model was the householder of one of these Eastern mansions, the Maronite Patriarch Paul-Pierre Meouchi. When I got to his palace he had not yet returned from the Vatican. A bearded old man with young keen eyes, the black Maronite hood pulled back over his head, was sitting in a dingy little room near the entrance of the palace. His fingers were cigarette-stained; he smoked constantly. His French was staccato and yet sing-song. A very young priest was joking with the old man as he served Turkish coffee. "He was only ordained yesterday," he said, pointing at the young priest, "and I am about ready to die." The keen eyes were having great fun. I pulled out my sketchbook and started to draw. "Let me put on my ring and my cross; I am the Father Superior here." The old man fumbled in a drawer.

The Patriarch came home, and the young priest guided me to a darkish salon through long rooms, all reddish and very oriental with low taborets and purple hangings and an aura of heavy perfume. It was moth-eaten and yet impressive; not exactly clean yet somehow well dusted. The little inlaid tables, the red velvet curlicued settee, the chandeliers, the low gilt-and-velvet stools with dachshund legs—how strangely familiar it all looked! Did I remember it from a previous incarnation when I may well have visited Levantine drawing rooms? Or did it return to me from some book or film long forgotten? Were there really peacock feathers in a vase on the ornate mantelpiece? Were there bearded patriarchs or odalisques in the ornate frames? Were there vases of perfumed artificial roses on a green marble pedestal with gilded grooves like a Doric column?

The Patriarch came in, tall and powerful, around seventy, majestic in his scarlet habit with skullcap.

"Voulez vous que je me mette ici, sur le divan?"

"C'est parfait, Excellence."

"Votre Béatitude," he corrected me kindly. Indeed, patriarchs are Beatitudes, cardinals Eminences, bishops Excellencies—*"Je vous demande pardon!"*

I liked his face immediately. It was severe and our conversation was accordingly most formal.

"Vous aimez Rome?"

"J'adore Rome, Votre Béatitude."

"Vous avez déjà dessiné beaucoup? Le Père Eugène me dit que vous avez fait un très beau

dessin du Patriarch Tappouni."

"Le Père Eugène est trop gentil, Votre Béatitude."

As time went by, his face became much less severe and tense. It had a certain mildness I noticed while drawing the left eye.

"Je connais très bien votre pays," he said suddenly.

"Vous connaissez mon pays, Votre Béatitude? Vous voulez dire la Hollande ou l'Amerique?'

"Les Etats Unis, je veux dire. J'y ai habité quartorze ans comme prêtre."

"But then you must speak English?"

"Sure do," he said with jollity. "Like the best of them! I used to live in Brooklyn, see, and in California, too."

He spoke Brooklynese with the perfect academic accent. His face was radiant now.

"Did you ever get back?"

"Sure. Last year I went all over the place. Boy, has it changed! I went all over the West Coast, too. I was the first Catholic priest to be photographed with President Kennedy!"—he pronounced it "foist"— "I had dinner with Vice President Johnson and his wife."

"You must have had a wonderful trip after so many years, Your Beatitude. What did you like best?"

The Patriarch thought for some time. Then his eyes lit up till he was all a-twinkle. "Disneyland," he said.

CHAPTER IV

❖

1982

❖

FROM

The Supreme Koan

Published by
CROSSROAD

THE SPIRIT

We may be living in the end-time of that eon which had its great flowering some twenty-five centuries ago, when in the span of three hundred years Lao-tzu and Chuang Tzu in China, the Buddha in India, Jesus of Nazareth in the Middle East, lived and died their answers to the perennial questions: "Who is Man? What does it mean to live this human life humanly?"

The Image of the Human, which they left to their contemporaries and to all the generations that followed, has remained vital ever since—or one should say until the deadly triumphs of modern nihilism. For as long as the religions founded on the mythical record of both the Christ and the Buddha—these pioneers, these mutants of a radically incarnational religious humanism—retained their vitality, the teachings and the lives of the Christ and the Buddha were the Lodestars by which the living could set their course, take their bearings.

Only a very short time ago, all that could be called "religion" had an aura of obsolescence and neurosis. In the last few decades there has been a sea change. After Vietnam and the disasters that followed, we may have lost some of our conceits. Not only are we no longer so uniformly boastful of inhabiting God's own country, but we have lost all illusions about glorious button-pressing utopias just around the corner. All our delusions of limitless progress by now seem to have evaporated a very long time ago. Our conception of the redemption of humanity by means of technological magic and gadgets will *in extremis* collapse.

Curiously, the idea of redemption, liberation, awakening has, as such, assumed a new urgency and new meaning, as if we were becoming aware that salvation might be that from our most destructive obsessions: liberation from our immense folly and suicidal callousness, a waking-up from the nihilistic nightmare of anti-values that dominates our world and which threatens our survival. We might just be recovering an awareness of our human condition, the wonder and awe that are at the wellspring of all spiritual life. D.T. Suzuki speaks of the so-called spiritual experience as being the experience of pain raised above mere sensation.

To paraphrase Lord Acton: Absolute *avidya, [sanskrit]* primal ignorance, delusion plus absolute power corrupts absolutely, becomes Absolute Evil.

CHAPTER V

2000

FROM

Pacem in Terris, A Love Story

Published by
CODHILL PRESS

During World War II, I served with the Dutch-East-Indies government in Australia, drew Australians, kangaroos and eucalyptus trees, and painted landscapes. I returned eventually to America and set up a practice in New York, at Thirty-Three East Sixty-Fifth Street with the emphasis on oral surgery. I never worked more than two or, if unavoidable, three days a week; I called it "my economic anchor." The rest of the time I drew, painted, and wrote in my loft on the corner of Bleecker Street and Sixth Avenue. It was the top floor of the two-story ramshackle building, still surviving, where according to legend, Edgar Allen Poe once sat writing. In 1953 my son Lukas was born. He was two years old when we took a boat to Europe, where I planned to draw and paint for at least a few months. In the ten days it still took to cross the Atlantic, I revised and corrected the manuscript of my first book, *Open Wide, Please,* a self-mocking "autodental biography," written by a Dr. Frank Fredericks, illustrated by Frederick Franck. It reached three printings in England, but I never published it in the States.

I was sure that I would never be able to decipher its messy, scribbled manuscript unless I could dictate it right then and there. At the Amsterdam Stedelijk Museum, while discussing my impending exhibition, I was given the phone number of a typist they often called upon when they needed someone who could take English dictation straight into the typewriter. I contacted her and started to dictate. It was on September 18, 1955, a record-breaking hot Sunday, and I suggested, after a few hours of dictation in her sweltering attic, driving to a beach close by for a few hours and continuing when it had cooled off a bit.

It was just a twenty-minute drive to Bloemendaal Beach, but before we reached it the sky had turned charcoal grey. The moment I stopped on the parking lot the thunderstorm exploded in full fury.

"Sorry, bad luck!"

But she sat there, eyes wide open as in a trance, staring ecstatically into the cloudburst, at the lightning flashes in the black sky.

"Ah! Look! Look! How beautiful! Mind if I go for a walk?" She had already kicked off her shoes and was out of the car, her long, thin feet trudging through the wet sand. All I could do was join her. Gulls dove into the wild surf, rose, staggered white-winged into the black sky.

"Ah! Look! See those gulls?"

She stood there, straight as a pine tree in the cloudburst, transfixed, pointing at the waves, the birds, the vertical flashes of lightning, her thin face streaming with rain.

"Such a gothic face!" flashed through my head. Van Eyck? Chartres? Reims? Anne of Aquitaine?

"Is your first name Anne?" I shouted against the thunder. She stood there in her trance, head tilted back.

"No! No! Claske!"

Friesian! Gothic! It fitted. *Coup de foudre,* or "bolt of lightning," the French call it, correctly.

"Do you know who you are?" I screamed against the thunder.

"What do you mean? Ah!" A huge gull shot by at eye level.

"Do you know who you are? You see as I see! Nobody, nobody ever sees what I see, as I see! You see! Never happened before. You are the one! We belong together, Claske!"

Soaked, we trudged back to the rented car, hand in hand. Rain was clattering on the roof, bolts of lightning hit the surf. Time stopped, time began.

> *expecting her to come*
> *how often*
> *have I wandered on the*
> *beach …*

says an ancient Japanese poem.

She had come! Life had started. Half a century later, we still walk hand in hand . . . .

•

I had a double exhibition on Madison Avenue, drawings at the F.A.R. gallery, paintings at Waddell's. They went very well. But at their end I stood there, looking at my canvases, semi-abstract, many of them jumbo size, sold and unsold, standing against opposite walls of the gallery.

Where did this work come from? Whose was it?

I knew for sure where my drawings come from: The hand follows obediently what the eye perceives. I let the reflex happen, let the tremors on the retina travel through every cell of my body on their way from eye—yes, via the heart—to the hand. The pen becomes the seismographic needle that traces the tremors on the retina. It traces a graph, and that graph is my drawing, as authentic as my thumb print, my DNA.

Painting—however intertwined it is with drawing—is a totally different process. The moment you pick up your brush, you become the latest in a line of predecessors that started somewhere in the grey past, via the Renaissance, then Cezanne. Here the line seems to have

split up, spawning one "avant garde" after the other, begetting the Fauves, Matisse, the Cubists with Braque, Picasso, the Surrealists, the German Expressionists, the Abstract Expressionists, until every brush-wielder of the 20th century, obsessed by the superstitious myth of "progress," had to try to do something really "New! New!" and, dizzied by cascades of influences, produced the potpourri of stylistic debris that chokes the galleries of Fifty Seventh Street, Madison Avenue, Soho, the Rue de Seine, and the Ginza, mirroring the nihilism that pervades our society. Zenith of the myth of "progress," or nadir of what art had aspired to, ever since Lascaux?

I stood there trembling.

What only yesterday I had been so proud of, suddenly filled me with shame, despair. I could have destroyed it all, then and there! The realization however destroyed the gallery artist in me forever.

What on earth had been the primal impulse that made me start drawing and painting so long ago? How did I get lost here?

Who is the artist-within?

The nineteenth-century French essayist Auguste Sainte Beuve wrote: "With every child a poet, an artist is born who dies young and is survived by an adult."

This short-lived artist must be the artist-within, the only authentic one who in some of us seems to survive against all odds. It is this artist-within I hold responsible for turning me into the compulsive image-maker who outlived the gallery artist, and who goes off the deep end if he cannot draw, paint, or make another steel icon for Pacem in Terris. If neither Cezanne, Matisse, Mondriaan, nor Braque were my patron saints, who were? Who else but those timeless, obsessed draftsmen whose eye was desperately in love with life, with the ecstasy of seeing: Rembrandt, Breughel, Durer, Goltzius, Guercino, Goya, Pascin, Kollwitz, Schiele, Klimt, Sengai, and Picasso at times, when he was not fooling himself and his audience. They had followed the irresistible impulse to draw what they saw, to let every line, every dot go through their every cell on the way from eye to hand. What all these compulsive drafts-men obviously had in common was the impulse to see, to see life first-hand, in constant wonder. Art had not been their compulsion to "self expression," to glorifi-cation of the inflated little ego. Art had been their zazen; draw-ing had been their tool, their koan to lay bare the core, to touch the Self, the Real in which we are and have our being.

I did not touch a brush for years, but drew as if my life depend-ed on it. It did! When, years later, I started to paint again I had for-gotten all about galleries, exhibitions, reviews. I drew and drew— and still draw—skies, people on New York streets, in museums, on beaches, in my native Holland, in Belgium, France, Italy, Japan, and Africa. When I draw from the car, Claske, at my side, is silent. She never disturbs me; she is all eye. She may silently point at something my eye might have missed.

The late Nanrei Kobori Roshi at Daitokuji in Kyoto, great callig-rapher and most revered friend, made me happy when he reassured me: "Yes, drawing is your zazen, you are a 20th-century Sengai!"

Around 1958, on a winter hike, we discovered the mortal remains of McCann's Saloon, a wreck that stood or rather leaned on the banks of the Wawayanda river in Warwick, New York. We fell in love with the spot, restored McCann's and have lived there happily ever after. Across the river stood an improvised garbage dump, in summer hid-den under a thick blanket of poison ivy, but once the leaves had fallen, it revealed itself to be enclosed in ancient fieldstone walls. It was the ruin of a late 18th century gristmill. It challenged me to restore it, to transform it into my work of art. A work of art outside of the art game, a trans-religious sanctuary outside of all religious games, a tiny sign of hope, a witness to what is still human in us humans. I called my oasis of sanity Pacem in Terris, Peace on Earth.

When, after a long absence in Rome, I saw our mill ruin again I knew in a flash how the roof, seen from every angle, would seem to fly away, the stone stairs from road level to the river's edge, the terrace to be built out of the mill's debris. I scribbled down what I saw in rough sketches that were not a groping for form, just reminders of forms that had come all by themselves, from nowhere. I already spoke of the project as "Pacem in Terris" when uncoding my scribbles with the young architect who translated them into prac-tical architectural drawings.

Bert Willemse was to be my only helper—apart from Claske, of course, who took the job that paid for Bert's wages and for the building materials needed. We would ask no one for advice, suggestions, or money. It would, for better or worse, be our work of art, our sacred space, our act of—unlabeled—faith.

The old mill had become my canvas. Freed from the rituals and delusions of Madison Avenue, life had offered me this second chance: to say in wood, stone, steel, and earth what had moved me from early childhood, deepened over the years of living through this cruel century. The gallery artist might have died a sudden death on Madison Avenue; but the imagemaker survived, was reborn.

Bert and I started at once to dig out the rubble and debris, twelve hundred wheelbarrows of it. We dug by hand, as machinery might have destroyed the old walls. Meanwhile, Bert had reinforced the jagged top of the ruin's walls with a beam of concrete and steel that tied the entire structure together. We continued digging until we reached the muddy pit where the mill wheels once turned. A millstone and a scoopwheel were rescued, as was the mill's axle—which was to become the trunk of the Tree of Life mosaic in Pacem's floor—a medallion of spikes, cogwheels, and horse shoes found in the rubble and set in concrete. We noticed how the pit kept filling itself with water although there was no connection with the river. It trickled down from springs in the rocks. "An omen!" Had not sanctuaries been built on sacred springs from time immemorial?

•

We swapped rocks from a wall between a neighbor's meadows for rolls of barbed wire. These rocks became the stairway from road level to the precious almost Romanesque archway and the paving of Pacem's floor. Bert started to assemble the gigantic fifty-one-foot-long diagonal wooden truss on road level. It would support the flying roof symbolizing the winging of the Dove. One day, returning from New York, we stood astounded. The truss was in place on its abutments.

"Rented a crane?" we asked.

"No," said Bert.

"Then how on earth did you do it?"

He shrugged.

"With the jack of my truck."

We were never able to get more information out of him. It remained the secret he took with him to his grave a few years later.

When I was not building, I kept working on the sculptures, the stained glass windows, the mosaics for Pacem, and I began to feel more and more closely related to the craftsmen of ages past: the masons, the wood- and stone-carvers, the icon-makers of centuries ago, the cathedral builders of the Middle Ages—even, all the way back, to those Cro-Magnons of Altamira and Lascaux who, thirty thousand years ago, painted murals on the rock walls of their caves.

It was as if I were taking a crash course on what the art impulse is really about: an art that is neither luxury, nor show-off, nor merchandise to be sold in those shops that call themselves galleries, and even less a hobby. Art must be something that arises from regions fathoms deeper than the empirical ego, from the deepest recesses of the human Spirit. It must spring from its maker's truth, his core, if it is to touch the core, the truth of the one who confronts it. Art does not seek to preach, to shock or to charm. It is not even too concerned about being liked. It can't help being what it is.

CHAPTER VI

1959

FROM

Days with Albert Schweitzer

Published by

HENRY HOLT/ROYAL FIREWORKS PRESS

I drove through a small town in central France in 1965 when my eyes fell on the newspaper headline in heavy type, "SCHWEITZER MORT." I grabbed the paper and read the flowery eulogy. It was replete with all the clichés common to the usual, sentimental Schweitzer rhapsodies.

The Schweitzer myth, however, must be neither shrugged off nor underestimated, for it is one of the very few positive, life-affirming myths of humanness and goodness born in this appalling time.

Here was the extraordinarily gifted son of a small-town Lutheran pastor who developed his immense potentialities to their utmost limit—as a physician, revolutionary theologian, as a profound yet practical philosopher, and as a great organist and musicologist who by the age of thirty abandoned his career as a full professor at Straszbourg University to start studying medicine.

•

The old man was sitting at his table, writing. His head, bent low over his note paper, nearly rested on the table. He muttered something, started to rummage in his papers, could not find what he was looking for, and muttered louder. His housekeeper-nurse-secretary, Mathilde, must have heard him, for she appeared in the doorway looking at the mess on the desk. Her hands folded she asked softly, "Were you looking for something. *Docteur?*" "Did I call you? Then stay where you are," growled the old man. Mathilde left meekly and Schweitzer went on digging in his papers. Then he got up, angrily. The old massive torso bent, the legs a bit curved in the frayed khaki trousers, the square bushy head thrust

forward. He started to leaf through the clusters of clippings, bun-
dled together with string, hanging from nails behind his desk. He
was still mumbling, found what he wanted, and lowered himself
onto the hard square stool ("I don't like chairs, I despise comfort").
He licked his fingers and leafed through the file of clippings.

Then he started to write again. His face was even closer to the
paper now, a face built around
a central massive core; the
large pitted nose as its base
and the heavy

brow-arch as its top. From it radiated innumerable lines deepen-
ing into grooves which divided the aged flesh into planes; above
his glasses the bushy eyebrows were knitting and un-knitting,
hairs sprouting and jumping over the rims. The line of the eye-
brows was repeated two or three times in parallel grooves on his
forehead. The skin looked hard, old, and element-beaten. The
white mustache bristled over his mouth and
nearly caressed the paper.

The old strong hand slowly,
deliberately wrote on. Then after a
sentence or two his head would
straighten and turn. For a few sec-
onds it would be fixed toward
the glassless window with its
mosquito screening and look
out over the river. Suddenly he
seemed to notice me again.
"Shall I pose for you?" he
asked kindly. "Oh, no,
please go on work-
ing, I'll sketch you
while you work." "Yes,
but not with my glasses," he
said, "they make me look too
old." Within a minute he had for-
gotten me and was writing again. It was
getting dark and the cicada music had

become as strong and irritating as a blaring radio. The file of ants marching across his table got out of focus in the falling dusk.

When he pulled the oil lamp toward him and lighted it, I noticed for the first time that he was wearing cotton sleevelets over his wrists so that the sweat would not soil his paper. After a few more sentences he got up again. He took the sleevelets off and put on a faded crumpled felt hat. "Let's sit down outside," he said.

I followed him out of the room and we sat on the steps of his porch, looking at the dusk deepening over the river. He seemed sad about something he had just read. "One should have the skin of a hippo," he said abruptly and without explanation, "and the soul of an angel." His dog Tzutzu sat between us. Mathilde came noiselessly behind us, standing erect with the toucan Jackie on her shoulder. It was peering at us from the beads on both sides of his ludicrous beak.

The old man looked at the evening and absorbed it. "Look at that tree," he said, pointing at a kapok in the distance, still caressed by the last light of day. We stayed, silent, a few minutes longer. The darkness had fallen quickly like a hood over the landscape. The dinner gong was sounding and kerosene lanterns started their dance to the dining room. He got up heavily, took his kerosene lamp from the shelf, and we all crossed the yard to the dining room. We put our burning lamps to wait for us in the little hall.

The twenty people in the dining room, who had been talking, became quiet and sat down. The last chair stopped scraping on the concrete floor. Schweitzer's eyes quickly darted up and down the long table, then they closed.

"Thank the Lord, for He is kind and His goodness is everlasting. Amen," he said quietly. During dinner I told him about a class of a public school in a poor section of the Bronx, where I had given a talk some time ago. The children, all thirty of them, had written letters to Dr. Schweitzer. "I just thanked them in your name," I said, "I guess that is all right." But the old doctor wanted to know all about it and I read to him some of the names— Spanish, Italian, Jewish, Polish, Chinese—and told him about the teacher who made it her task to teach all these white, pink, yellow, and black children to get on together. He looked at me with suddenly very young eyes under the bushy white eyebrows. "But this is important," he cried out, "this is *really* important!"

After dinner he asked me to his room and I watched him write with his old hands slowly and steadily two letters, one to the children of P.S. 53 in the Bronx and one to the teacher:

> *…I myself come from an old Alsatian family of schoolmasters. My grandfather, his four brothers and two sisters were schoolmasters. And I, deep down in my heart, am a schoolmaster and have a schoolmaster's soul. That is why I understand so well your work in the difficult and very special profession of a teacher!!*

CHAPTER VII

1961

FROM

African Sketch Book

Published by

HENRY HOLT

GARDEN PARTY AT LASTOURVILLE

We were aloft already and there was the Ogowe river, the Schweitzer Hospital, and the god-awful jungle, stretching endlessly; the stink, the heat, and the anxiety were almost unbearable. There would be three stops before Brazzaville. At the first stop some Africans got off to go to their villages and a few white passengers joined us. The second stop would be Lastourville. The plane touched down and made a sort of jolly jump on what is called a runway in this part of Africa. We piled out as the chickens and goats scattered before the invasion from outer space. Dinner-jacketed gentlemen and their ladies and many others clambered into a truck which served as the local limousine service.

We sat in "Meteo," because there were a few chairs and a bed. A few minutes later Madame "Meteo," very pretty and young, walked in with a child at her breast. She sat down to complete the feeding, smiling at us. Only then I noticed that this was not a waiting room, but the bed-sitting-drawing room of Mr. and Mrs. "Meteo." Mr. "Meteo" also came in soon, sat down, and said, "Well, you'll have a long time here."—"More than half an hour?" I asked. *"Ah, oui, monsieur,"* he said, "maybe tomorrow"—he had the beautiful ivory smile of Africa—and went on, "I have just radioed to Brazza." "But what's happened?" I asked bewildered. "Something wrong?" "But didn't you notice? You smashed two wheels of your landing gear coming down."

I went out and saw indeed there were more people standing around and under the plane than usual; for on an African early-sixties airstrip there are always a number of unauthorized visitors watching the proceedings of fueling, loading, and unloading, a few of them with lighted cigarettes in their mouths. There was very little left of two of our three wheels and the jolly little jump at the landing might well have been our last one.

The answer that came back from Brazza obviously said that it *was Sunday and "que voulez-vous?…C'est la période des vacances."* But tomorrow morning they would send a plane to pick us up. Nobody was excited. The eighteen passengers merely shrugged their shoulders, and the captain found a bottle of whiskey. We sat in our dead plane, waiting for the flight engineer to come back from his explorations in the town of Lastourville, about five miles away.

Back at the plane my fellow passengers were still drinking whiskey. It was stifling. I sat down and read an old *Paris-Match*. The captain looked a little less grim after his third whiskey. "Do we sleep in the plane?" I asked him. "Maybe," he said. "We have two DDT bombs," the steward consoled us pleasantly. "I know," I said, because they had fallen on me during the jump. There was the sound of a jeep in the distance and the navigator came back. He had a bottle in his hand, "with the compliments of the Commissaire de District," who was also trying to arrange lodgings for us for the night. But it was difficult, for Lastourville had only four European families. There was plenty of space for the African passengers, however.

Another truck arrived and we were taken to the heart of the village. The road went downhill, past the huts I had already seen, and kept on going downhill for five hundred feet, through a dark funnel of dense virgin forest. Then all at once we were at the end of the funnel: a vast valley spread out below, with the wide Ogowe River winding through it and rows of mountains receding into a blue background behind it, as in a medieval painting. Deep down in this Shangri-La a few neat houses formed a circle; in front of the biggest one were two flagpoles with the French and Gabon flags flying in a lazy wind. We drove through a little Arc de Triomphe of trained trees and in the open doorway of the white, flower-bedecked bungalow stood the Commissaire de District. He was a fat man, smiling happily; he had a pipe in his mouth, and a slightly wry neck on high shoulders gave him a quite aristocratic appearance. He wore a dark green sweater and said simply, *"Soyez les bienvenus,"* adding, "won't you join me in a drink on the terrace?" as if this had been a carefully arranged garden party to which he had been looking forward. His servants noiselessly passed whiskey, crème de menthe, and Heidsieck champagne. Three immense palm trees had their roots deep under the terrace, from which one could see the blue-green vegetation going down steeply a few hundred yards to the river's rocky edge. Below, the river was calm and a pirogue drifted dreamily toward the distant wild rapids. A little farther downstream the waters divided to embrace a high island, a patch of virgin forest which must have swarmed with a complete collection of African fauna. My eye followed the river to the bend, where it disappeared in a horizon of golden haze.

On the terrace twelve people, who had yesterday never suspected each other's existence, were drinking champagne together in a fantasy which had lost all contact with reality. The conversation was general and forced. Only the Commissaire de District belonged here and he found it so commonplace that he did not even show off his house, which was open on all sides to the coming evening.

Next to me sat a French-speaking American missionary, who had nothing to say. On my other side was a Texaco dealer from deep in the *brousse,* who looked like a French Gary Cooper. He felt obliged to throw a few words of broken English in my direction once in a while. A surly, tall Commissaire de District from somewhere, was mainly interested in the gun collection of his colleague. A garage owner from Brazzaville told us the gruesome details of the intertribal riots: how at the roadblocks passers-by were simply asked: "What tribe?" and if the answer happened to be wrong, they were quickly decapitated. He described with relish how pregnant women were cleanly disemboweled. The young director of a new radio station and his tired-looking wife concentrated on their cherub-like baby for whom the whole adventure did not yet exist. A lumberjack with a lean

medieval face spoke in a very strong French patois and made jerky wooden gestures. The captain of the plane had put on a leather jacket and kept silent. An African journalist in a blue serge suit was talking softly with a French Jesuit missionary who looked like Jean Gabin.

Our host tried to entertain us with topics which in his opinion would interest everybody, mainly hunting stories and particulars about the African customs of his region. But the animals interested him more. On his walls were beautifully framed pages from Buffon's *Histoire naturelle,* and most of the books on his shelves were about animals. "Animals are my passion," he said as he got up, lightly for such a heavy man, and waved us to the buffet which had been prepared.

And here, hundreds of miles away from the next settlement, in a funnel of virgin forest, on a large mahogany table covered with damask, waited an exquisite *buffet froid.* "You were unexpected, and I am sorry but you will just have to take potluck," smiled the Commissaire, waving his arm toward *caviar Mallosol, pâté de campagne, foie gras, thon à la portugaise,* and thin slices of cold roast beef. There were freshly fried potato chips and many more complicated and tasteful things and warm fresh French bread. There was an endless supply of mellow Bordeaux and a particularly fruity, cool Moselle wine.

Had the plane really miraculously made so safe a landing? Or had we already ascended to some afterlife, standing around a table, piling plates with delicacies in front of wide open doors, with the soft murmur of waterfalls below and a too esthetic crescent moon over the palm trees?

After supper we returned to the terrace, and more drinks were served. In the stillness of the equatorial evening we were all enveloped in irreality.

"How long shall we still be tolerated on this continent?" mused the priest, sipping his cognac. "I don't know," said the Commissaire, "but I wouldn't know what to do in France, that I can tell you." "They'll still need us for a long time to come," growled the Texaco dealer. "They aren't reasonable enough to see that," said the radio man. "Their leaders know that they couldn't operate a radio station, that they couldn't drill the oil wells, that they haven't one single economist. But the young hotheads think they can do everything, because they are completely ignorant, and the Russians will try to confirm them in their beliefs and take over."

"We don't want to exchange a mild tyranny for a harsh one," said the African journalist. "We know very well that we got an education from you, that without your engineers, technicians, and doctors we are sunk. We need you administratively, medically, technically. But then, I am a moderate and I know it."

"Yes," said the Texaco man, "you know it. But still you want your 'independence,' don't you? And expect us to pay for everything, fill the gaps in your budget, defend you, and give you every service for free. Do you think that can go on forever? What is your press doing to make it clear to your people how much you need us? If we get out, you'll go back to the jungle in a few years' time. Look at the Congo," he said triumphantly, "I am told that Leopoldville is already beginning to be overgrown with jungle." "You'll start eating each other again," the lumberjack joined in viciously.

"I think we won't," said the journalist quietly. "We know it will be difficult, but we have men of good will. We are divided in tribes and we cannot sweep away the old customs. But we have more than we ever had. We have French as a common language, we can communicate with each other. We want a civilized way of life, even the village people want it. Maybe they don't quite know yet what efforts it will demand of them."

"And your politicians won't tell them either," said the pilot, mixing in for the first time. "They are just fighting about who will get the greatest power, the biggest car, and the most trips to Paris or the United Nations."

"They will learn. And our people will learn to distinguish between them," the journalist replied. "Our people are tired of being black sub-proletarians. They feel the need to live like other human beings. You have taught them that need, if you have taught them anything." "We may have taught you many needs," said the priest. "Maybe you were better off before we came. We have taught some of you in order to make you clerks in our offices and mechanics for our Caterpillars. But we have failed to raise the level of the family, for how few girls have we trained? It is true, your people haven't cooperated very much…Now you want bicycles, radios, and sewing machines and cameras, and you think that is culture. And I'm afraid you'll sell your soul to whoever promises 'things' to you."

"You are thinking of the Soviets again, *mon Père,* said the journalist with a smile. "I grant you that where there are frustrated, discontented politicians and poverty-stricken populations the Communists have their chance. But we don't want them. The Chinese Communists have done fantastic things in the few years they have been in power,

but we don't think their example could possibly work in tropical Africa. On the other hand, I grant you that we want the things you have. We want housing, food, hospitals, and education, especially education. But above all we want human dignity. You never gave us that, did you? You took it from us. You don't mind doing things for us. But never with us. You despised us really. Now we want to build our countries ourselves, for we have learned that we are human beings like you. If anything, more human than you."

For a few moments nobody spoke. Then the priest said, "What I worry about is that you have no tradition of responsibility except to your clans, you have no tradition of the brotherhood of man except within your tribe, and we have not been able to instill it in you."

The African smiled again. "Aren't you a bit optimistic about the honesty of your own politicians? And your European history, as I read it, is not exactly a demonstration of brotherhood between your tribes."

"If you ask me," said the doctor, who had previously remained silent, "we are all in a mess. I love this country and I get on splendidly with the people. But very soon you'll throw me out. I think the tragedy is that there is not an evolution, a slow movement toward real autonomy, but just this disease of 'independence.' And you Africans grab for that as a child grabs for the moon. I don't believe you people are inferior to us, I won't even believe you are so different. I think you have magnificent qualities, extraordinary vitality, great potentialities. But I feel that all Africa has been infected by a virus which we have brought to you: nationalism. And this virus has driven you mad, it has given you delusions of grandeur and the belief that through a new magic you can stamp your foot

French II's People waiting

and conjure up a society which can equal the old European society. But European society was not built in one day; it was based on long traditions of thrift, husbandry, investment, and inventiveness."

The journalist opened his mouth as if to speak, closed it again, and shrugged his shoulders. There was a strange cry from below. The Commissaire got up and nodded to me. He took his flashlight and some fruit from the table and I followed him below the terrace. A large baboon sat there on his scarlet buttocks and started to run excitedly in the circle allowed him by his leash. The Commissaire talked to him and the baboon sat down again, his large round eyes focused on his friend, who gave him a banana.

"You can talk about Africa until you are blue in the face," he sighed. "There is no such place as Africa. There is no common ground between the peoples of the Congo, Ethiopia, and Sierra Leone. There are hundreds of languages in every administrative unit. There are differences of soil, of climate, of religion, of customs. All it has in common are dark-skinned people with curly hair and protruding lips and the terrible infection called 'independence,' as the doctor says."

"Maybe there are some other things they have in common," I said. "They are not created equal, as little as we whites are created equal, although I believe absolutely that all of us—black, white, yellow, and green—are created equivalent: of equal human value. I agree with the journalist that Africans have in common a sudden realization that they are human, and

they long for human dignity. And with it comes the absolute resolve to share in the resources of their countries, and to share fairly. And a hope to better themselves. Their self-confidence is confirmed every day by those kinsmen who have reached positions of prominence and power in the world." "Assuming that you are right," said the Commissaire, "what will it mean to us?"

"Nothing easy," I replied. "We shall have to accept that all we have ever injected into Africa will be transformed beyond recognition, whether it is Christianity or democracy or perhaps even medicine. They will make it African and it will be different, compounded of old and new, theirs and ours. Not a mixture of both heritages, but a new compound. If this new product frightens us and we cannot accept it, we shall lose the continent spiritually, politically, and economically, and it will seal our doom, for Africa is awake now."

My host was petting his friend the baboon. The moon had disappeared and a hot, heavy breeze was blowing. On the terrace the guests dozed over their drinks…

"Is Africa really awake?" the Commissaire said, pouring himself a last cognac, "or do we whites just think so because we are fast falling asleep?" He looked at me with a bitter smile and lifted his glass.

"Happy dreams, *mon ami!*"

CHAPTER VIII

1976

FROM

The Book of Angelus Silesius

Published by

VINTAGE/BEACON POINT PRESS

When the poet, Angelus Silesius, talks about human fate and foibles and of his firsthand experience of what lies beyond, when he speaks about ego and what lies beyond ego, he is a radical for whom God is the unknowable Mystery, Nothingness, Abyss. Here the Zen Master would understand him perfectly. Are they perhaps speaking in different words of a very similar experience?

The Silesian mystic stood in God's presence during his four days of ecstasy. The Zen Masters simply stood in the Presence, in the Present, in the Now/Here. Both must speak of their most momentous experience, as if to tell us: Trust your deepest intuitions! You are not alone! You are not mad! You are not losing your way! You are your way.

•

In my own search for That Which Matters, I found in Zen, so many years ago, a full confirmation of my intuition that I, like every other human being, contain a hidden but incorruptible core. It is hidden underneath immense layers of confusion, neurosis, delusion. Yet it is our true center. It is our truly human nature. It is our very core of sanity! The sayings of the Zen Masters speak of this core in a variety of terms: Bodhi, Suchness, Self-Nature, Buddha-Nature, the Original Face, the Essence of Mind, the True Self, the Unborn, the True-Man without-label-in-this-mass-of-red-flesh.

Might this True Self not be what in Christian language is spoken of as "The Light That Lighteth Every Man That Cometh into the World," "The Inner Light," "The Kingdom Within," "The Birth of God in the Soul," "The Indwelling Spirit"? Could Christ be the

Master who summons man to find the True Self, and his Sermon on the Mount the self-revelation of Enlightened man and the values he lives by?

It is more important to realize that we are born in complete ignorance of who and what we are, (avidya) and what it really means to be human. If our lives are to be lived as human lives, we have to discover our fundamental and specific humanness. The question is: How to discover it? Is it true, as one is often told: "You can't learn it from a book?" It depends on which book and how you read it! I have learned more from the right book (and the more right it was, the more often I had to read it) than from the most famous guru…To find the right guru, teacher, or spiritual guide is about as difficult as to find the right spouse or even the right plumber…

Zen is: escape from the Me to the True Self. From illusion to Reality, from the madhouse into sanity.

Zen is: Life that knows it is living expressed inwardly and directly, without adornment—in art, religion, love, humor.

Zen is: seeing the world, my wife, my cat, myself not just as they are, but such as they are.

Zen is: that which joins what our rationalizations have torn asunder, and tears apart what they have joined.

Zen is: time experienced as timelessness, eternity. And eternity as time, as now/here.

Zen is: where the commonplace is no longer banal but won drous, where the natural is perceived as just supernatural enough: "How miraculous, I draw water, I carry firewood! I blink my eyes! This skeleton dances, it talks, makes love!…"

Zen is: the living life in me, aware of itself as the life in its impermanence and mortality that is shared by all beings.

Zen is: discovered—after long preparation—when it reveals itself in a flash of insight.

On the flyleaf of a book I found something dated August, 1955, scribbled in the lobby of a four-star hotel in Europe when I was kept waiting by some personage who, at that moment, seemed important enough to wait for:

"I walk naked in my clothes, within my skin.
That which looks through these eyes and watches,
        is from eternity to eternity watching itself
        motionlessly going through the motions."

"What is the Buddha?" the emperor asked the sage.

"He is not far from where your question is coming, Your Majesty."

The organized religions, whether Judaic, Catholic, Protestant or Muslim, have throughout history been frightened by those mavericks who insisted on having their religious experience firsthand and who proclaimed that the "repository of truth" is to be found only in the human heart.

At best they were shrugged off and pigeonholed as "mystics." At worst they were hanged, burned or quartered according to local preference…

It is as if Angelus Silesius had invented his own Western haiku

and doka to express his mystical experiencing of the Real. His vers-
es are hardly longer than those of Ikkyu, 13th century:

"How marvelous, how god-like the mind of man.

It fills the whole universe! It enters every mote of dust!" says
Ikkyu.

Angelus Silesius answers with:

"How this heart, no larger than my hand,

can enfold heaven, hell, and this wide earth—

This is the mystery no man will ever understand."

> *"Do not compute eternity*
> *as light-year after year.*
> *One step across*
> *that line called Time:*
> *Eternity is here."*

> *"How short our span!*
> *If you once realize how brief,*
> *You would refrain*
> *from causing any beast or man*
> *the smallest grief, the slightest pain."*

> *"Unless you find paradise*
> *at your own center,*
> *there is not*
> *the smallest chance*
> *that you may enter."*

> *"De profundis,*
> *my heart cries out*
> *to the divine Abyss.*
> *Which of the two*
> *the deeper is?"*

> *"When challenged to explain*
> *the Absolute*
> *I shall fall still,*
> *I shall be silent as a mute."*

CHAPTER IX

1992

FROM

To Be Human Against All Odds

Published by

NANZAN UNIVERSITY PRESS/
ROYAL FIREWORKS PRESS

THE THREE SAGES

Whenever I have met true humanness, and it has happened often, I have been moved, often to the point of tears. Each time it has been a revelation to see it in a mere gesture or a glance, to hear it in a word spoken at the right moment. At times it was as if I had a built-in manometer of which the needle at once moved from the B of "Bully" or "Beast" to the M of "Mensch," which in my native Dutch—as it does in German and Yiddish—means "human being," regardless of gender, and for which, tragically, English lacks a single word.

After long hesitation I had dared to request a brief appointment with Daisetz Teitaro Suzuki. For some ten years I had studied his books, ordering them from Rider's in London as they had not yet been published in America. On a single sheet of paper I had jotted down what I thought I had understood from his writings. I just had to know: was it all nonsense or not?

"May I read this to you, Professor Suzuki? Only please tell me whether it is all nonsense."

"Go ahead," he nodded. And so I read what I had written down. An extraordinary smile appeared on the wrinkled face. "It is not nonsense."

I got up, thanked him, mumbled excuses for encroaching on his time, and made to leave. But he gestured me to sit down again.

"May I ask you another question?" I ventured. "People often ask me what Zen is. What would your answer be?"

"I would say, Zen is that which makes you ask that question.

When you ask, 'What is Zen?' you are asking 'Who am I ?' and when you ask 'Who am I?' you are asking, 'What is it to be human?' It is the existential question, the primal riddle we bring along into the world when we are born and must answer before we leave it, on penalty of having gone through life in vain."

"Zen is not a religion," he went on, "it is the profoundly religious ingredient in the world religions."

"And the rest is folklore?" I asked.

Once again he smiled. "Come and see me again."

I never did have the nerve to infringe once more on the precious days that remained to Suzuki at his age. He had confirmed the clue to the one great riddle: the Zen of being human, Zen as being the closest contact with the innermost workings of life inside and around oneself.

Daisetz Suzuki died at ninety-six. His most poignant essay, "The Unattainable Self," he wrote at ninety. Years later I visited his grave in Kamakura. As I stood there, I could see him smiling. "Nice of you to come, but I am not under this piece of rock." Or, as Ikkyu (1394-1481) wrote:

> *I shall not die*
> *I shall not go away*
> *Just don't ask me any questions*
> *I shall not answer.*

In the late 1950s and early 1960s, I served on the medical staff of Albert Schweitzer in Lambaréné, Gabon Republic formerly French

Equatorial Africa. At age thirty-two, already a celebrated organist, full professor at the University of Strasbourg, author of standard works on theology, Johann Sebastian Bach, and on organ building, he gave up everything. He had vowed that it was his vocation to allay human suffering. He studied medicine and in 1913 started to build his jungle hospital in a part of Africa devoid of all medical help. For decades he supported his hospital by giving organ recitals in Europe—I heard him play Bach in Haarlem's ancient St. Bavo in Holland when I was twelve. Between hernia operations, obstetrics, and leprology Schweitzer found time to write his level-headed philosophy on scraps of waste paper gathered on hooks above his table.

He was then deep in his eighties. Yet at six in the morning I listened to him practicing Bach toccatas and fugues on his zinc-clad tropical piano with organ-pedals. He played with an intensity as if he was scheduled to give a gala concert in his jungle that day. He insisted on being awakened in the depths of night to supervise some emergency operation by one of his young doctors.

For the reporter from *Time* magazine who tried to draw him out on theological questions, I translated his curt dismissal, "Dogma divides, the Spirit unites."

On a photograph he gave me as a keepsake, he wrote in German:

> This is the island in the Ogowe near the village of Igandja,
> 80 kilometers downstream from Lambaréné, where on a
> September day of 1915, I had the revelation that the principle

of Reverence for Life is the ground of any viable ethic.

Regarding the third sage, Angelo Roncalli, the son of poor peasants who was to become Pope John XXIII, I can be brief. When I read his opening speech to the Second Vatican Council he had convened—it was on October 11, 1962, I recall, in the midst of the Cuban missile crisis—I was so struck by this vox humana coming out of the Vatican, that against all reason I flew to Rome. I simply had to respond as the artist, the image maker I happen to be. I simply had to draw this event, which I felt sure would be "a watershed in the history of the human spirit," far beyond the confines of the Church.

Against all odds I succeeded in gate-crashing the tightly closed shop of Vatican II (1962-1965) and was able to document the four sessions of the Council in hundreds of drawings. On June 3, 1963, Pope John died. Once again I flew to Rome to draw this extraordinary pope, this genius of the heart, one last time on his bier. I had seen in him the embodiment of the wisdom that is compassion, the compassion that is wisdom, the prophet of human solidarity in our time. I saw him as a Christian Bodhisattva, who on the threshold of death wrote in his last encyclical "Pacem in Terris," "Peace on Earth," "God has imprinted on man's heart a Law which his conscience enjoins him to obey."

It was unheard of. A pope who spoke about a law imprinted not merely on the paper of holy books, but directly carved into the human heart itself! It could only be the Great Law, the Dharma, of the specifically human, of being human against enormous odds. He was a manifestation of the Spirit in my lifetime.

•

"THE AWAKENING"
STONE CA. 6"0"

BIOLOGICAL CRITERIA OF BEING HUMAN

In the many scientific papers he published over the last thirty years Paul D.MacLean MD, Chief Emeritus of the Laboratory of Brain Research and Evolution at the U.S. National Institutes of Health formulates and elaborates his concept of the hierarchic structure of the contemporary human brain as being a "veritable trinity of brains." In this "Triune Brain," the central core is the surviving reptilian brain. It is enveloped by the old (paleo-) and the new (neo-) mammalian brain. These reptilian and mammalian components were clearly differentiated structurally, functionally, histologically, as well as chemically by Dr. MacLean and his co-workers.

The reptilian core, *still very potently active in us,* already some 240 to 280 million years ago knew all it needed to know for mating, breeding, flocking, grooming, migrating, and fighting. It was even adept at rituals of greeting, challenge, aggression, and submission. Its courtship rituals were acted out in accomplished choreographies, with dazzling displays of color added for sex appeal. Timetables for the routines of daily life were also part of this reptilian brain's repertoire: breakfast at eight, lunch at noon, happy hour at five, bedtime at eleven, so to speak.

Without touching on problems like the correlation of structure and function, one is struck by the quantum leap that occurs in the transition from reptile to mammal. The young, who are ignored or even devoured by reptiles, are nursed by mammalian parents. A capacity for play evolves together with parental care.

Vocalization appears in the form of the still non-verbal "separation call" which connects offspring and mother.

Correlated with the much enlarged olfactory apparatus, the marking off of territory by body odor and urine deposits appears. In contrast to reptiles, who are slaves to precedent and ritual, mammals show the capacity to memorize more critically, "creatively." They can adapt to changed conditions by changing their responses. In humans this "creative" adaptation reaches its peak: humans are *"learning animals."*

In the great limbic lobe—which the brain of all mammals have in common—MacLean has located specific areas concerned with self-preservation, feeding, fighting, but also with emotional and socio-sexual aspects of life.

The neo-mammalian brain continues to mushroom into the twin hemispheres of gray matter of the neo-cortex to form the superb intracranial computer that makes the human brain capable of deductive reasoning, calculating, learning, and verbalizing.

In the human brain, however, intracranial communication is handicapped by having a trio of deficiently connected control-processing centers, of which the two older ones, the reptilian and the paleo-mammalian, are inadequately "wired" and "programmed" for transmission of the symbolic signalings of language.

Possibly stretching the point, MacLean speculates about the jurisprudence of our legal systems as possibly having its most ancient antecedents in the reptilian fidelity to habit and ritual. Could there possibly be some remote connection, for instance, between those universal human signs of awe and submission—kneeling, bowing, inclining the head—and the millions-of-years-old reptilian rituals of submission? Could something of the reptilian rituals of challenge and aggression perhaps have survived, hypostatized in the characteristics of "military bearing," and in that "goose-stepping" which is all too similar to a lizard's, a crocodile's rituals of challenge?

The greatly expanded capacity for communication of the human neo-cortex, far transcending the still non-verbal "separation call," eventually results in speech. Language makes the verbal expression possible of much that remains unarticulated by the reptilian and mammalian components.

The remarkably expanded intracranial computer of our neo-cortex is relentlessly logical, inflexibly rationalistic. It seems to be relatively devoid of intuition and feeling, and as such it does not yet merit to be regarded as human. Could it be this still pre-human reptilo-mammalian computer that is responsible for the ruthless ways in which we humans manipulate, exploit, abuse, maim, and decimate members of our own species and despoil our environment?

Could its apotheosis be the H bomb, Auschwitz? Could it be the intracranial computer which is steering our Spaceship Titanic on its collision course with a Reality beyond its ken?

Contemplating life's mysteries, Chuang-tzu (500 BC) mused:

> One may well suppose the True Controller to be behind it all. That such a Power works I can believe. I cannot see its Form: it acts, but has no Form.

The *Heart Sutra* says, "Form is Emptiness, Emptiness is Form." The Western mystical poet Angelus Silesius might have had a similar hunch in the seventeenth century:

> *God the Formless*
> *makes himself as Form*
> *becoming structure, substance*
> *lightness, darkness*
> *stillness, storm.*

Immersed in Mystery as we are, we might as well indulge in the fantasy that either nature, or God, or Plato's *anima mundi*, or Chuang-tzu's True Controller bethought itself a few million years ago, having created a miniscule Frankenstein bound to destroy not only itself—a sustainable loss—but all of this little planet and all that lives on it, and perhaps eventually to destabilize the entire cosmic order.

Either this or some other enigmatic, preordained evolutionary force must account for a mysterious, crucial, and relatively recent phenomenon, which enriched the mammalian neo-cortex with its newest, latest, most momentous outcropping—the Pre-frontal Cortex that would act as a corrective on the merciless computer.

The prefrontal cortex, connected as it is with the limbic system, endows us—according to MacLean's data—with novel capacities such as the capacity for unprecedented awareness of our own the impermanence life process, which by itself differentiates us from all our predecessors on the evolutionary ladder. This in turn seems to enable us to feel the first stirrings of *empathy,* of identification with the life process of other living things, a responsiveness to the needs, the suffering, the "rights," of other beings.

From empathy to *compassion* is but a step. The prefrontal cortex also makes *foresight* possible, perhaps as a first inkling of causality. Is it the dawn of our capacity for imagination?

In short, the prefrontal cortex seems to function as a merciful, life-enhancing corrective to counterbalance the ruthlessness of the intracranial computer. The awareness of our life process, the capacity for identification with other life processes, empathy, compassion, foresight taken together seem to initiate the specifically human capacity of imagination.

The Human has taken its bow on the evolutionary stage.

CHAPTER X

1993

❖

FROM

Zen Seeing
Zen Drawing

Published by
BANTAM BOOKS

MEDITATION IN ACTION

You can "look-at" things while talking or with a radio going full blast, but you can see only when the chatter stops. Among all the letters from readers, this one was different:

"I have read every one of your books. They are precious to me, not because I have learned so much from them that was new to me, but because they reminded me again and again of what I somehow know, but constantly forget."

•

The Buddha is quoted as saying: "We do not learn by experience, but by our capacity for experience."

I appeal to this capacity for experience, to our capacity to see instead of to look-at. This capacity is the essence of the artist-within.

Who is this artist-within? The French essayist Charles Auguste Sainte-Beuve wrote, a century ago: "With everyone born human, a poet—an artist—is born, who dies young and who is survived by an adult."

A contemporary thinker, Rudolf Arnheim, concluded that "every child entering grade school in this country embarks on a twelve-to-twenty-year apprenticeship in aesthetic alienation. Eyes they still have, but see they do no more."

Two much more ancient quotations belong here, for they touch the very heart of the matter. The first one dates back to seventh-century China, when Hui Neng, the Zen sage, said: *"The Meaning of Life is to See."*

Not to look-at, mind you, but to *see!*

Another of these ancient Chinese, Hui Hai, reminded his contemporaries: *"Your treasure house is within; it contains all you'll ever need."* This bears repeating amidst the din of television commercials for all the trivial things we don't need!

No wonder that once the art of seeing is lost, meaning is lost, and all life itself seems ever more meaningless: "They know not what they do, for they do not see what they look-at."

"Not seeing what they look-at" may well be the root cause of the frightful suffering that we humans inflict on one another, on animals, on Earth herself.

The experience of seeing/drawing showed me that art has very little to do with the fabrication of salable products, of gallery merchandise, that art is not a drag race between avant-gardes with bets placed on the winner. Art is the most profound, most irrepressible response to life itself, whether that art is drawing, dancing, playing a flute, or acting on a stage. Seeing/drawing is, for me, that response, the response of the artist-within.

•

One day I was drawing a cow in a meadow near our house. As I stood there drawing, our eyes met, and at that instant she stopped being "a cow." She had become this singular fellow being whose warm breath condensed with my own in the cold fall air. We were standing eye to eye. Who, what was looking from her eye into mine, from mine into hers? Her big moist eye shifted. Slowly she turned around. My pen followed. When I checked what had appeared on my paper, it struck me forcefully that what I had drawn was nothing other than the subject matter that had inspired my Neolithic forebears when they drew such bovines on the walls of their cavernous living rooms. I was back at the cradle of the artist-within everyone!

Something in me had jumped back to a moment before history began, had freed me from all of history's permutations, swept aside all of Greek, medieval, Renaissance, and modern art, dismissed all the influences of all those generations of artists that preceded ours and conditioned our seeing. It was as if they had never happened! I had drawn this sister cow directly "from life"! I had drawn life as this eye-of-my-own had perceived it! I had leaped back thirty centuries to the very Origins.

Seeing/drawing must be my way of practicing Zen. Fundamentalist Zennists may scoff at this and question its validity as Zen practice.

I myself had some doubts, until many years ago a revered Zen master, Abbot Kobori Nanrei Roshi in Kyoto, reassured me completely. He confirmed that "seeing/drawing" is obviously *my* Way of practicing Zen, an artist's Way.

Seeing/drawing, my meditation by eye and hands as one, has never become a routine. When I start a drawing, I have no inkling of what the outcome will be. I'll never be a "professional."

•

Zen is the breakthrough from the Me to that True Self, which is also pointed at as the Buddha Nature, as "the True Man without rank (or attributes) in this hulk of red flesh," as the Indwelling Spirit.

INTERMEZZO IN KYOTO

On my dozen or so trips to Japan I was deeply touched, almost shaken, by the first Noh Play I saw in Kyoto's Kanze Theater. Noh is the classical theater of Japan. Asked whether it is like Kabuki I can only say that to me the difference is that between "The Merry Widow" and Bach's B Minor Mass.

Noh derives from a folk theatre in the Middle Ages. It included dance, acrobatics, mime and music. Even in Kanami's (1333-1384) time it was still popular theater for the entertainment of the common people during temple festivals. Its tempo was twice as fast as it is today, its style realistic and free. Only after Kanami's son, Zeami (1363-1443), at eleven years old, became the protege of the Shogun Ashikaga Yosimitsu and grew up to become Noh's greatest actor, playwright, and choreographer, did Noh begin to assume its present form. Until that time the status of Noh actors was not much higher than that of beggars and street jugglers. With Zeami, Noh found itself suddenly raised to the dignity of a court ceremonial and its actors to posi-

tions of quasi-equality with samurai and even high nobility. Noh quite naturally adopted the value system and the code of manners and of honor belonging to its patrons, to become an aristocratic art. It developed the extreme stylization of emotional expression, which governs its diction and its choreography. Every movement, the simplest action—walking, sitting down, getting up—became ritualized. Naturalistic gesturing and posturing were scorned. The extreme interiorization demanded utter exertion of all the forces of the actor's body and soul, so that ideas and feelings might shine through the imposed restraints by distilling and purifying themselves to most concentrated essences. There is no place in Noh for deviations or improvisations, or for the actor's idiosyncrasies. Attempts at "originality" are not tolerated. In Noh, if anywhere, the artist is clearly compelled to make the choice between self indulgent originality and the authenticity of the Self.

The Shite, the bearer of the action, as well as the Waki, who is his foil, must empty himself of all "self-expression," becoming one with the personage enacted. Yet, paradoxically, a great Noh actor makes visible the uniqueness, the authenticity at the core of every human life.

The function of Noh is catharsis, reconciliation with the "angst" and pain of our existence, awakening us from our delusions. Strange as its style may be to us Westerners, Noh is no stranger, no more a riddle, than the human heart itself.

In this theater, so deeply intertwined with Zen attitudes to life,

it is indeed transmission from heart to heart that is intended and achieved, transforming the spectator into the concelebrant in this so very Japanese and yet so very universal liturgy of human authenticity.

Maybe we have arrived at a point, now that so many are once more in search of meaning and human values at which we can absorb the essence of the Noh experience. This is what Noh signals to me and so I sat for days on end in Kyoto's Noh theater, absorbing and drawing the liturgy of the Human called Noh.

The French diplomat-playwright Paul Claudel wrote: "In Western theatre something happens, in Noh someone appears," and Jean Louis Barrault, the great actor and mime, saw Noh as "the avant-garde theatre of the future."

On a blustery November day, when I stood waiting on a platform of Kyoto station for the Shinkanzen, the bullet train to Tokyo, my eye was struck by three elderly Japanese. Two women were sitting on a bench, an old man on his haunches in front of them. They were eating sushi from cardboard lunchboxes. A few yards farther away, at the kiosk, students—the boys in their black school uniforms, the girls in the usual navy blue sailor suits—were kidding around, buying sodas and things to nibble. I was struck suddenly, very deeply, by this banal scene. It was as if I watching some miraculous supernatural pantomime. I itched to draw it, but the train was to pull in at any moment for its precise two-minute stop. Still, without realizing it, I must have unscrewed the cap of my drawing pen, for sud-denly I felt my hand starting to move all by itself. It flew over the paper of my little sketchbook in precise synchronization with what my fascinated eye perceived. I did not have a split second to glance at what appeared on that paper. The pen kept on gliding, leaping, dancing, from the old people on the left—it even touched some lit-tle figures in the background—then jumped to the students on the right-hand page, and back. The train came to a stop. I hardly man-aged to put my pen away, grab my bag, and leap just in time. The automatic doors closed barely behind instead of in front of me. The train picked up speed. Within seconds, factories, buildings, flew past, then hills and pale green rice paddies, forests of smokestacks, a thousand high-tension pylons. Still shaky, out of breath, I sat down. It took a little while before I dared to look at what that pen had thrown down in those few seconds on the paper. It seemed impossible! How could this have happened in no-time? I was delighted but felt frightened at the same time. Was I dreaming?

I was definitely not dreaming. It was as clear as it was wonderful and a bit scary: All inhibitions had evaporated, as if at long last—at eighty-some I had put full trust in the eye-heart-hand reflex. I had let the pen do its work with-out meddling, without suspiciously checking whether it was doing its job properly. The reflex had simply func-tioned, without my interfering with it. The artist-within had taken over the controls.

The seeing/drawing that, in Africa, I had discovered

to be my second nature, had become first nature. This "first nature" sat here drawing Japan from this speeding bullet train, as if I had lived here forever. From alien territory, Japan had turned into home ground, one of my multiple home grounds.

For while seeing/drawing—I had been aware of it before—time may expand and contract. A minute can contain an hour, an hour may shrink into fifteen seconds. Inner time becomes totally disconnected from linear time, clock time.

"The seeing have the world in common," Heraclitus had noticed a few millennia earlier. The lookers-at, the onlookers, the voyeurs have been killing, torturing one another ever since, and are still at it.

I flew to Europe. In alleys of the red-light district of Antwerp's harbor, the pen at once started to scribble down the half-naked women and their clientele. "No comment, no moralizing!" said the pen. "They are such as they are."

In the Pelikaanstraat, center of Antwerp's diamond trade, the Hasidic dealers stood gossiping, haggling, negotiating, as an entire previous generation had stood there before it was carted off to the gas chambers. Drawing these survivors, not understanding a word they were saying, I heard them proclaim what we humans make known uninterruptedly, what I have heard them broadcast in every language I understand. I have even heard it quacked by ducks, roared by lions, and clucked by chickens: "I want!" "I like!" "I adore!" "I despise!" "I hate!" "I love!" "I am!" "We are!" "You ain't!" "They ain't!"

Only what is really seen, experienced, lived, becomes part of the Treasure House within. "I click my shutter, therefore I am," tolls the death knell of the artist-within.

Seeing/drawing is the antithesis of this snapshooting. The whole person is committed. Far from being a hobby, it is a total openness to that which meets the eye. It is: to be in touch with the Ground of Being, inside and outside of oneself.

In seeing/drawing the entire concentration—for a change—happens to be on That which is not-Me, on that rose, that face, that ruin that fills the entire field of my consciousness.

I know some people—they are few and far between—whose eye is so fully awakened that their artist-within needs neither pencil, brush, cello, nor Steinway. They simply live the artist-within! Their very glance, their slightest touch transmits the fullness of life. They are the salt of the earth.

A true drawing is never a show-off piece; neither is it ever intended to be a public document, and even less a piece of merchandise. It has as little ulterior motive as breathing.

Since in seeing/drawing you "become" what you draw, it makes you comparatively harmless.

Accused of "caricaturing" the bourgeoisie of the Café de la Poste, anywhere in France the *grand bourgeoisie* of Café Hermitage, the *haute bourgeoisie* of the Caffe Greco in Rome, I plead not guilty. I do not caricature these people. They caricature themselves! I see them as I see myself: ephemerals on their brief trip from and to nowhere. I see their social masks as I see my own, that self-confident, amiable, lighthearted mask, that infallible mask of the doctor in his office, the dignified mask of the man on the rostrum, the makeup of the lady in the mink. I see them in their naked vulnerability, for I have drawn naked bodies from life for forty years and have developed an X-ray eye that sees through all the shenanigans, the furs, the lace, the poor devils underneath the finery. The pen does not mock, it hallows.

> "What is it that dwelleth here
> I know not
> but my heart is full of awe
> and the tears trickle down."
> —*11th century Japanese*

Old ones, unenlightened but sane as they are, are often wise enough to sit on benches in parks practicing the Zen precept: "When you sit, sit; when you walk, walk. Just don't wobble."

•

When the Emperor of China asked the great Bodhidharma to explain the sacred, the sage shrugged.

"Nothing sacred, Sire, just a vast Emptiness, unlimited openness!"

When I first read this, I daydreamed that—after a profound obeisance, of course—I dared to mix in: "Venerable Sir, you said 'nothing sacred.' Couldn't that perhaps imply that *all* is sacred, these mountains, rivers, the whole great earth with all that lives on it? And would this not make us guilty of constantly, uninterruptedly committing sacrilege against this sacred earth and its inhabitants, humans included?" Bodhidharma remained silent, but the emperor muttered: "Sacrilege…uninterruptedly…" He repeated it a few times.

Then he spat at me: "And what would you, impudent scribbler, do to stop being so uninterruptedly guilty of this sacrilege? Answer! Or I'll have your head amputated!"

"Sire," I heard myself say, "what else could I do than to continue what I did today?"

"And what *did* you do today?" the emperor hissed.

"I drew these humble weeds this morning, Majesty. They are only called weeds of course: These beings that grow out of the Great Emptiness must have their sacredness. And this afternoon I drew this old woman, Sire, in her nakedness, her sacred dignity after a long life of child-bearing, of boiling rice, scrubbing floors."

"Hm!" grunted the emperor. "And what made you think of this highly original way of interrupting the 'uninterrupted sacrilege,' may I ask?"

"I did not think of anything. I just saw the weeds and the old woman. Perhaps, Sire, it was just the overflow of the *kokoro*, of the heart…Come to think of it, Sire, I really do not need my head very much."

"Oh well," said the emperor. "Neither do I, so keep it!"

•

In Greenwich Village the rain came splashing down on Braque-sienna brownstones. Diamond bubbles exploded on red, black, and mauve umbrellas. A dull charcoal cloud deck weighed down on the grimy gleam of roofs. People stood sheltering in doorways, staring into the wet dimness. They, the rain, the bubbles, the mirrorings in puddles were orchestrated flawlessly. Everything was exactly where and as it ought to be, in precisely that half-light needed for

HOLLAND

heartrending beauty.

Sun broke through the dense clouds. On the sidewalk in Little Italy, in front of a leprous "Democratic Club," four old men, two gesturing on rickety chairs, the other two stamping around, joined in a passionate debate. The pen may be mightier than the sword, but it is less mighty than the assault rifle, and so in New York—rain or shine—I draw from my flimsy space capsule. I stop the battered old cocoon at a hydrant; wait until it becomes an almost invisible detail of the streetscape. Only then do I start scribbling in the little sketchbook on my knee.

•

.....I spotted her on Fourteenth Street. She was selling wigs, and to promote her merchandise she wore an outrageous sample on her own head. It made her look like Medusa. But when, as my pen started its scribbling, I caught her eye, I saw how convinced she was that her headgear had transformed her into an irresistible Venus of Milo, with arms and legs emphatically restored. For a second or so, this Venus cast her spell on me. Then the X-ray eye came into action and broke the sorcery. I finished my drawing, equanimity regained.

•

On Canal Street, in the drizzle, I saw a large old man approaching. I would have taken him for a prominent lawyer, a Republican senator or corporation president in his slightly stooped distinction, if he had not worn a faded Hawaiian shirt and carried a plastic bag and a battered little folding table of mottled aluminum under his arm. He set up the folding table, took five little toy dogs out of the plastic bag. He found an abandoned crate and sat down heavily, staring into the

drizzle, making the little dogs dance, and waited.

In his drawings Rembrandt proves beyond all argument how independent the inner dimension, inner space, is from size. Each one of his postcard-size Holland landscapes is a precious lesson: Those few square inches suffice to embrace the fathomless spaces of the universe.

In the wintry gloom of another war that—as wars will do—came inexorably, I looked out of the window and saw our white rabbit, fancying itself a snow hare. Coal-black eye afire with delight, it was jumping crazy capers in the falling snow, white on white.

Again, "Splendor of the World" flashed through me, and I mused that it is this Splendor—without Why—that had kept me drawing through most of this century of agony.

•

Butsugen, in the eleventh century, said:

"You monks, straining day after day to understand what Zen might be, are barking up the wrong tree! What you can't seem to see is that *all* is beyond understanding, not just one thing or many things, but every single thing is fundamentally beyond our understanding. The Really Real in its Suchness is beyond our understanding. Just *see* it in this light."

Seeing it in this light, I see/draw, I draw what is beyond my understanding, That Which Matters, the Really Real, is right before my eyes!

It is not hidden!

Seeing/drawing is more than making pictures: It is witnessing to this seeing, it is touching the Meaning beyond understanding.

One day I saw that the sun was round
Ever since I have been the happiest man on earth!

•

The artist-within is the one who sees and witnesses to this seeing: whether in the great ones, in Bach, Rembrandt, Piero della Francesca, Rilke, or in us lesser ones, even very little ones…

Wherever I go
I meet him
he is no other
than myself
yet
I am not he.
　　　　—Dosan

What shall I leave behind
empty skies
fields
grasses
dandelions
sparrows swarming
faces, faces
each one veiled
each one mirroring
the Face of faces.

CHAPTER XI

1978

FROM

The Death and Life of Everyone

Published by
DOUBLEDAY

We are beginning to realize that to get out of our nihilistic trap we must dare to reinvent a "religious" attitude to life—our own, our fellow men's and that of the Earth itself. And so countless people everywhere seem to be launched on a new spiritual search, which—if authentic—is none other than the quest for Reality.

In the individual the spiritual search is released and activated by pain, the pain caused by the collapse of our delusion that "this can't happen to me." It is this inevitable crisis in each human life—the collision of the ego and its delusions with the blank wall of Reality—which leads either to cynicism, to the deadness of resignation and stagnation in the prehuman phase or... to "rebirth." Rebirth *(metanoia)* is a wholehearted saying "yes" to life on the fully Human plane of insight...

I see the "new" religious attitude to life now emerging as the realization that, not only individually but as a species, we are on a collision course with the Structure of Reality as such, with the Laws, *(the Dharma)* which rules the life process of the Earth and of humanity. There is a desperate longing at the eleventh hour for a new harmony between the cosmic and the human life cycles, for the resacralization of what has been willfully desecrated.

This "life of the spirit," always born in the solitary human being, is never confined to that solitary one, for to be truly awakened is to be aware that the others are as real as oneself, their suffering as real as one's own. Hence, the awakened spirit is unable to ignore the great social dilemmas of our time—war, hunger, the mutilation of the earth. It sees these dilemmas for what they are: at least as much "spiritual" problems—that is, "Reality" problems—as practical, political, or technological ones.

We are by now all too familiar with the technological solutions of "practical" men: genocide as practiced by the Nazis, ecocide as it is committed by the industrialized countries, and collective suicide as it is being brilliantly prepared by departments of "Defense," in collision with multi-national corporations.

•

A Sunday morning in Kyoto. It started with my taking part in a Shinto service. The most sacred gesture consists in either two or four handclaps, according to whether it is an ancestor's spirit, a kami who is invoked or a god who is called down. The worshipper, kneeling, head bowed, gives these gentle claps and then his hands remain joined together in silent prayer. I am always deeply moved by this quiet reverence of wordlessness, and although not a Shintoist, I have often participated in these Shinto services, quite naturally, feeling almost at home.

Afterward, walking through Kyoto, I entered a Catholic church. It was the moment of the elevation of the Host. People were kneeling, their eyes closed, hands clasped together under lowered heads. Others entered on tiptoe, sprinkled water in an act of purification almost identical with the one at the animistic Shinto shrine. A man crossed himself slowly, pensively. His sign of the cross was a hieroglyphic sign: an invocation of the Human, of the Sleeping Christ within.

That afternoon we drove to Uji to see the ancient Buddhist temple of Mampuko-ji. Here there was no God to be worshipped, but Sutras were chanted, interlaced with solemn gong beats. Monks sat on round cushions, eyes half closed, hands folded, thumbs touching. The abbot repeated profound bows at the main altar.

Walking out of the temple grounds of Mampuko-ji, I saw in my mind's eye Moslems prostrating themselves in noonday prayer, Hassidim swaying rhythmically, chanting, Sufi dervishes whirling, the devout at Guadeloupe with arms raised as in Byzantine ikons…

While watching all this folding and clapping and clasping and joining of hands, this chanting

and raising of arms, this closing of eyelids and bending of spines and knees, this whirling and swaying, all this holy gymnastics flowed together in one sacred dance. The awesome choreography of withdrawal from all distraction, from all that changes and shifts, a turning toward the still Center, the Unborn-Undying. It was as if it caused a short circuit: preventing the escape of all energies to their habitual outward busy-ness, making these energies into wordless signalings from the heart to its Ground, compelling the Ground to answer. I saw it as a sign language that must be part of our physiological make-up, inborn gestures of reverence, of prayer, that are our most intimate means of contact with the deepest layers of the Self, of the Sacred that is everyone's ground, released when in joy or pain we are overcome by its fascination and awe. Beyond all doctrines, all theologies, these are gestures of the Specifically Human.

I stood in that Japanese temple garden and felt myself surrounded by the 125 million Japanese who crowd these narrow islands, thirteen times as densely populated as our own country. I was acutely aware of my being an expendable, interchangeable atom in the ever-expanding population on our earth, overawed by the realization that however many of us there may ever be born, each one will be Everyone, each called to attain the Truly Human, the True Self, or will have been called to life in vain. Each one contains the fully human potential: the "True Man": the unassailable Magna Carta of his human dignity.

•

I thought of the agnostic humanism of my parents' home. Theirs was still the optimistic faith in the humanness of decent, good people, based in their naïve trust in the sweet reasonableness of human beings, unable to imagine what our ghastly century was to reveal. They were agnostics but not nihilists. They

honored all the life-affirming values. My father was no atheist. He honored the All-Encompassing in awareness of his inability to grasp Its nature. "I try to live so that if there should be a Judgment, I would not have to fear it." This he not only said, but lived. His imagination was not perverted enough to visualize the utter horror of the nationally and multinationally structured evil that was to dehumanize humankind and finally threaten to drag it down into collective suicide. He died at fifty of pneumonia in March 1933, just before Hitler grabbed power.

CHAPTER XI1

1981

FROM

Art as a Way

Published by
CROSSROAD

Born innocent, one
—that's I—
strives hard to become
an adult, no longer childish,
worldly-wise
in one's art, one's love,
one's life...
Then discovers:
that no one ever
becomes an adult,
becomes either
delightfully childlike
or pitifully infantile...
Discovers:
one's art to be outside of the art game
one's faith beyond the religious game
Discovers:
one's own little song
and at last dares to sing it
in all variations,
unsuited as it may be
for mass communication...
For perhaps
here and there
someone will hear it
and listen
and know
and say
Ah!
Yes!

There was a time when the simplest utensil, the lowliest earthenware bowl, testified in its beauty to those qualities of the spirit which are at the wellspring of all living cultures. The ugly had not yet been invented…

Art did not yet, self-consciously, present itself as "art." It was not yet the busyness of gallery exhibitions, opening galas, of curator-critic-dealer cartels, auctions and art columns, with all the shenanigans of a too affluent society. It was still intertwined with, unseparated from, life in the human mode.

I don't just glance at Rembrandt's nudes…The moment I begin to scribble his Suzanna, his Hendrikje Stoffels in my sketchbook I stand there and let my pencil follow what my eye sees. I am not "copying," I am making contact. I no longer see these women only through my eyes, but also through the Master's. Both Rembrandt and his women spring to life! Scribbling down his self-portraits I share the painter seeing himself as the proud young artist, then deeply saddened in middle age, finally alone and old as if crushed and shrunken in an empty universe.

That I speak here of art as a Way, implies that I see the way of the artist as a kind of pilgrimage. When you go on a pilgrimage, you set out from where you happen to be and start walking toward a place of great sanctity in the hope of returning from it renewed, enriched and sanctified.

However far you may walk, every pilgrimage is a safari into your own dark interior, an inner journey. For pilgrimages belong to the inner world, to that realm called "the religious."

There are, of course, innumerable pitfalls on the inner journey;

a great variety of mountebanks and charlatans, from commercial gurus to bigoted fundamentalists have their traps baited for the spiritually starved…

Once upon a time—as I see it now—I was an "artist"… But then this "artist" died suddenly, and I found out that maybe I just belonged to some species of compulsively image-making animal, and I understood Ryokan's saying—slightly paraphrasing that 18th century master: "Three things I dislike: poems by a poet, paintings by an artist, cooking by a chef."

If we say that man is made in God's image, it must mean that he is born a creator: image maker, myth maker, poet. From his authentic subjectivity authentic art springs forth, in our time as in that of the cave painters of Lascaux and the tellers of the myths of antiquity. This is the art that never loses its timeless freshness, its perennial validity.

No generation before us has had such powerful means at its disposal not to be. This lost capacity for experience, for openness to Being, has produced brand new forms of barbarism

Rembrandt's late self-portraits show an old man with a bulbous nose, disabused eyes, wrinkled skin. But what makes these portraits so disturbing and unforgettable is that here the "True Self" in Rembrandt was obviously contemplating the "Me" already gone to pot, in detached serenity, without a trace of self-pity.

It is as if he pointed at the face in the mirror to say: "This is it and nothing more!…Ecce Homo! See the human condition!…" This is the art of Rembrandt in his later years: profoundest meditation on the human condition.

So, what is art?

No one has ever defined satisfactorily anything that really matters, be it art, love, God, life itself…Still, what art might be I learned one day, while driving along an endless straight road. I had switched on my radio. Station after station blared its pseudo-news, wretched demented chatter, jingled shameless commercial lies between its horror stories, burped the cacophony it calls music… Vexed and exasperated by this tidal wave of putrescence, I finally turned the knob to stop the torture. I had turned the wrong knob…

And there, suddenly, against a sky of harpsichords and oboes, arose a clear, limpid voice singing a Bach Cantata. The Human Voice! Tears sprang into my eyes. The human voice at last! We humans can do more than produce gadgets and garbage!

This too was made by one of us humans!

Since then I know beyond all argument and debate what art is: *Art is that which, despite all, gives hope!*

A Bach Cantata, a Mozart string quartet, a Schubert sonata, a haiku by Basho, some little drawing by Rembrandt, Goya, Pascin…and faith in the human, almost abandoned in despair, is totally restored.

•

Art then is that which contributes, however minutely, infinitesimally, to the regeneration of our world.

CHAPTER XIII

1965

FROM

My Eye Is In Love

Published by
MACMILLAN

In this activity of eye and hand combined, I have found that there is an inexhaustible well of joy. At a time in which we and our world are threatened by total, instant destruction, I have learned to dive into the reality of my life by drawing. I also find it to be an act of worship or, perhaps, conjuration. I drew the grasses behind a motel in Vermont, a nestling human habitat in Brittany, the vineyards around a house in Provence, the low Holland sky seen from a train, a mountaintop from a terrifying old propeller plane over Ethiopia, and each time I felt in absolute contact with the center of life, fearless, filled with joy. In the hubbub of New York I drew faces in a park, a dying man in a hospital ward, people in a subway—and in doing so came to say yes to the baffling city. The majestic rocky coast of the Pacific while drawing revealed its transiency, and a baboon facing me in the Congo spoke of eternity: I drew rock and ape in joy. Wherever I drew and while drawing, I became part of, I participated in, and identified with, my world. Instead of worrying about the bomb, I began to learn to live with it. As long as in drawing I can still say yes to the city, to the shells and the beaches, to a jungle path in Nigeria, I say yes to life. In this book I want to communicate the joy of the magic incantation that is drawing.

My drawings are certainly not offered in competition with the masters of prehistory or those of the seventeenth, the nineteenth, or even the 20th century. Without apology they are offered as one man's way to draw and to come to terms with his existence.

Sometimes the relevance of art to the problems of our time is called into question. No wonder. The whole epoch is focused on technological achievement, busily realizing dreams of interplanetary weekends. The art produced since Picasso and Joyce (both drawing on inexhaustible resources of an unbroken culture) dared reject all preoccupation with tradition. The artist with the infatuated eye then may appear as an anachronism, his non-utilitarian eye as obsolete as a horse-drawn streetcar. Yet obsolete or not, my eye perceives and sets the hand in motion. Thus for certain human beings, graphic symbolization of their perception is still an integral part of the process of living and of the fulfillment of their potentialities. There is the absurd question sometimes asked by pedants, "Has art after all brought anything of value since Holbein?" ("Since Rembrandt? Since Renoir?") They believe that art is a making of things, instead of a process integral in certain individuals, a process that results only incidentally in triptychs, cathedrals, and oratoria. Because the root of art is Epiphany: the estatic delight at the realization of being alive, being able to see and to feel. If the art of our time is kaleidoscopic, it merely reflects the confusion of values, the bafflement facing the breakdown of the symbolic universes of traditional religion and traditional science.

In seeing/drawing, the whole person is involved: the eye perceives, intellect and feeling are taut. A reflex arc goes from eye to hand through the whole body and somehow through all that is called mind and heart. All the hand does is precipitate a line, provided it obeys perfectly and is not interfered with by the meddling, cheating ego. All progress in drawing is the exercising of the reflex arc and the short-circuiting of "creative" little Me. All the hand has to be is the unquestioning seismograph that notes down the pulsation, the meaning of which it knows not. The less the conscious "personality" of the artist interferes, the more truthful and personal the tracing becomes. True drawing is always original in this sense, but it is a kind of originality only perceptible to the aware observer, not the kind of originality that the ego strains for.

During the act of drawing, a sleeping homeless man, Albert Schweitzer, a gull, a pope, a flying pelican, a cabbage and a cardinal, a leaf of grass become equivalent.

In drawing, I become aware of, part of, even identical with, all that passes before the steady eye.

The more I strive for "originality" in drawing, the more it eludes me, the more trite the product becomes. We are so afraid to be ourselves that we are rarely authentic, and in straining for originality we are bound to copy. It becomes a mannered handwriting, part of some convention or other. It becomes pseudo drawing, in which self-indulgence and the addition of what may seem interesting devices addle the privacy and truth that are the essence of the act of drawing.

The contact needed for drawing is not merely visual. It is total, and it establishes immediate and reciprocal relationships. Wherever I have drawn, in the harbor of Accra, St. Peter's Basilica, in leper villages in the Congo, or in native huts in

Ethiopia, I have made friends. Human beings and even animals have reacted to the absolute concentration and acceptance that were part of drawing them. Children in African villages immediately recognized what I had drawn: human eyes totally untrained in art appeared to be able to read those symbols of ink on paper instantly, naturally, without effort. I once heard a famous nonobjective painter say, "I want to see the way a primitive bushman sees, not as concept but as sheer perception."

I was enchanted by the revelation that these children of the jungle villages who had never seen art or an artist in their lives, interpreted spontaneously the lines and dots I was making as an image of their world. They confirmed that I was handling a universal language, the same language that may have been old when the bulls were drawn in Aurignac, some thirty thousand years ago. Standing in a grotto in Lascaux, I had the feeling "Here are my true ancestors!" Life has not changed except in nonessentials. Life and death are still with us. There is no doubt that there is a future in this kind of drawing, if human life continues on earth. There is a future in this pictorial communication with self, which, incidentally, communicates with a Bantu child, a girl in the subway, a schoolteacher, or with luck, even a collector. To draw is not only joy, it is at the same time struggle, tension and despair. But, more important, it brings the artist liberation from compulsive concern with "style," from spurious originality, from worry about "being of one's time." Drawing unconstrainedly, I cannot be anything

but myself, product of my time as well as of my culture, my whole heredity. In the eternal stream of forms I am just one, the one who must note them down.

•

We were driven out of Paradise, but Paradise was not destroyed." —Franz Kafka

•

I have sat down to draw in the old port of Marseilles, in the camel market at Omdurman, on the beach of Moclips, Washington, on the steps of a church in Mexico, in a dugout canoe on the Ogowe River. One thing these places have in common, I learned: they are all on earth! This may be an obvious truth, but every truism is a platitude until it becomes a living experience. While drawing, I discovered that everywhere under one's feet are the pebbles, the sand, the mud, and the sparse or opulent weeds and grasses. Everywhere in the distance the forms coalesce, bathed in a haze, drowned in a glare. The whole vision may be enveloped in soft and humid vapor, in limpid morning light, or in boiling, trembling heat. Some of these atmospheres are part of one's hereditary structure and draw themselves.

I grew up in the vaporous, rainy atmosphere of Holland, and somber, rainy days when everyone is grumbling; these fill me with deep contentment, a feeling of being at home. Home remains where the eye first opened to perceive and love the world. Fatherland is to me those four or five square miles where I roamed in childhood and experienced the miracles of light, of earth, water, and trees. It is where I suddenly felt each tree growing from its own roots, the life force pushing itself upward, twisting and turning its branches against invisible pressures and resistances.

•

I look at a church emptying. People parade in their finery, they irritate me with their primitive display. Suddenly the irritation switches to sadness as their clothing seems to melt away and they shuffle around the town square naked, pitiful, suffering from corns and stomach ulcers, their knees bent in rheumatic pain. I take my pen and draw the young in their brief display of smooth fitness, the middle-aged, already tired and obese, the old ones limping on their crutches. The pen no longer caricatures, mocks and guffaws, it weeps inconsolably.

Then again while I scribble an El Greco self-portrait in the museum, people pass in front of me and become suddenly as fascinating as the painting I have come all the way to study. The pen jumps from El Greco's beard to his miraculous "View of Toledo."

•

There are thousands of miles in America, Europe, and Africa, which I have "done" by car. Nothing has meaning in my memory except those places where I got out of the car to sleep or eat and wandered around for a while. Between New York and San Francisco all I remember are little patches of earth behind a motel in Pennsylvania, the spot where I had a flat tire in Ohio, the pond where I went swimming in Emporia, the roadside where I felt sick in the San Joaquim Valley. All the rest, all the "splendors" looked-at while driving, all those panoramas, lakes and mountains have faded away like cheap picture postcards.

•

"Tenderness is not weakness," Chardin's still-lifes prove. "Nor is freedom nihilism," add the Rembrandt drawings.

The Rubens sketches teach that spontaneity is by no means sloppiness. Goya demonstrates the gulf that separates passion from convulsive loss of control. Uccello proclaims that strength is not brutality. Ingres shows that chastity and frigidity are not synonymous. Guardi proves that vitality is not violence and Fra Angelico that joy and mania are not at the same but at opposite poles.

•

If you take up a paintbrush, you cannot dispense with drawing without missing the very wellspring of art, one cannot attain freedom of expression without drawing oneself to freedom. All shortcuts mean the acquisition of a small bag full of tricks on which to depend: heads à la Klee, hands à la Picasso, monstrosities à la Bacon, drips à la Jackson Pollock. Dead-end alleys.

The pen, even more than the pencil, refuses to flatter one's vanity. It demands a steady hand, coordinated with a clear eye.

Without pity it shows up all flabbiness of purpose, the slightest flagging of concentration. The pen is not only mightier than the sword, it is even mightier than the brush. The pen

is even mighty enough—for who dares answer its challenge?—to cure the paranoia (delusions of grandeur and persecution) so easily unleashed by brush-wielding. Note: few people afflicted with paranoia have a desire to be cured, and there is little inducement, for every paranoiac has his paranees, who just can't wait to confirm his delusions of grandeur and even feed them. These paranees may bring fame to the patient if he is an artist, or a following of Sturmtruppen if he is a politician.

•

Near Menton I draw an old olive grove. It is so old that its trees no longer bear fruit. They have the terrible strength some women have after they are done with the business of charming, marrying, and childbearing; they have the invulnerable beauty that becomes theirs after the mating-mask that nature lent to them has withered away.

In that grove I have drawn for days. Each one of these olive trees shows that through its many years it has struggled with all the forces of wind and lightning and rain, all the angels and devils of the tree world. Each tree has lost a few limbs in the struggle but survived. Its roots have grasped the earth as tentacles, as claws, as legs, as feet; its branches and its trunk read as a compendium of all the forms of nature. The grove at Menton would be my favorite place of exile. Within its square mile it would offer me the human and animal body in all its unending variations; there is not a single form of foot, or breast, or buttock these olives do not have. There is not a mountain, a cloud, a hillock, or a sea monster whose form cannot be discerned in the roots, trunks, and branches of these venerable trees.

Last year driving in Provence, I was drawn to these olives… they had disappeared. One of them was still standing in front of a large, posh, off-white and chartreuse mansion and there was a sign in its front yard: "L'Oliverai," "The Olive Grove."

Where there are no nudes to draw, I draw trees. The limbs of apple trees move as if crushing weights block their every movement toward sky and light. The tree's every contortion is testimony to giving in to, yet circumventing, the oppressive forces in order to overcome them triumphantly. Suddenly the young shoots burst cheering toward the sun, straight as the sun's rays, answering them, meeting them, and sucking them into themselves.

Apple trees are universes, a naked one in winter, a blushing one in bloom, or one bearing fruit in that dazzling, confusing richness of branches and leaves, which the mind cannot encompass nor the pen adequately follow.

CHAPTER XIV

1973

FROM

The Zen of Seeing

Published by

ALFRED A. KNOPF/VINTAGE

Who is the artist in us? The unspoiled core of every one before choked by schooling, training, conditioning until the artist-within shrivels up and is forgotten. Even in the artist who is professionally trained to be consciously "creative" this unspoiled core shrivels up in the rush toward a "personal style," in the heat of competition to be "in."

That core is never killed completely. At times it responds to Nature, to beauty, to Life, suddenly aware again of being in the presence of a Mystery that baffles understanding and which only has to be glimpsed to renew our spirit and to make us feel that life is a supreme gift. Many years of preoccupation with Zen have kept me awake to the experience of this opening up of life.

In this 20th century, to stop rushing around, to sit quietly on the grass, to switch off the world and come back to the earth, to allow the eye to see a willow, a bush, a cloud, a leaf, is "an unforgettable experience."

We do a lot of looking: we look through lenses, telescopes, television tubes. Our looking is perfected every day—but we see less and less.

Never has it been more urgent to speak of seeing. Ever more gadgets, from cameras to computers, from art books to videotapes, conspire to take over our thinking, our feeling, our experiencing, our seeing. Onlookers we are, spectators. "Subjects" we are, that look at "objects." Quickly we stick labels on all that is, labels that stick once and for all. By these labels we recognize everything but no longer SEE anything. We know the labels on all the bottles, but never taste the wine.

Millions of people, unseeing, joyless, bluster through life in their half sleep, hitting, kicking, and killing what they have barely perceived. They have never learned to SEE, or they have forgotten that man has eyes to SEE, to experience.

I have learned that what I have not drawn I have never really seen, and that when I start drawing an ordinary thing I realize how extraordinary it is, sheer miracle: the branching of a tree, the structure of a dandelion's seed puff. I discover that among the Ten Thousand Things there is no ordinary thing. All that is, is worthy of being seen, of being drawn.

It is a discipline of *pointed mindfulness* as such, persevered in to the point where the in-sight breaks through. Zazen may be the discipline of Zen, but I, for one, am not good at sitting still for long in the lotus position. I believe that in *seeing/drawing* there is a way of awakening the "Third Eye," of focusing attention until it turns into contemplation, and from there to the inexpressible fullness, where the split between the seer and what is seen is obliterated. Eye, heart, hand become one with what is seen and drawn, things are seen as they are—in their "is-ness." Seeing things thus, I know who I am!

•

There is the story of the Buddha holding up a flower to his disciples and asking them to "say a word about it," something "relevant." The disciples looked, looked intently, then tried to outdo one another in the profundity of their remarks. Only Mahakasyapa remained silent and smiled an almost imperceptible smile. To see is Mahakasyapa's smile. But why a flower? Why not a dead rabbit? A minnow? A poor old soul?

When all the antennae are out, as they are in *seeing/drawing,* the eye perceives, and a reflex goes from the retina, via what is called "mind" or "heart" to the hand. In *seeing-drawing* all the hand does is trace a line, to note down the tremors on the retina as an unquestioning instrument. All doubt, all fear, all pretensions have been banished.

Such drawing is "personal" in the sense one's fingerprint is inevitably personal. It is "original" in the way the ancient Chinese used this word: it is "in harmony with the origins."

While drawing a rock I learn nothing "about" rocks, but let this particular rock reveal its rockiness. While drawing grasses I learn nothing "about" grass, but wake up to the wonder of this grass and its growing, to the wonder that there is grass at all. If you can see, you can see with your nose and smell with your ears. Gregorian chant has the scent of incense. The fragrance of apple blossoms can be seen: soft whitish-pink with the golden light of spring.

•

As a circus horse I have had to make desperate efforts to place my hind legs where the trainer so obviously wanted them. I tried to please my trainer. I wanted to avoid the whip's gentle reminder, which I felt more as a reproach than as pain… As an old cart horse I have felt dull and heavy, pulled my load in listless resignation. Yes, I have been a donkey, too…with extreme and distressing frequency… although I enjoyed carrying children on my back…

•

Drawing the naked body shows up every incompetence, every sloppiness, but especially every infantilism, vulgarity, lovelessness, callousness, of the person who draws. All peeping, all looking, all non-seeing, non-feeling, is caught red-handed. Show me your "nudes" and I know who you are…

As I am writing this, gnats, moths and mosquitoes, fatally attracted by the mini-sun of my desk lamp, fly to their death. I try to chase them away, shade the lamp, but they persist in their suicidal urge toward the light.

I am drawing an old man. He seemed to be sleeping peacefully, and yet as I drew I noticed how all of him was in constant motion. The hands on the counterpane opened and closed, his eyelids contracted and relaxed, his chest heaved, his nostrils jerked, his cheeks were drawn in and blown out. Then, suddenly, my hand stopped. The sleeper had stopped moving. He had died.

Everything moves ceaselessly until the moment of death.

When drawing a face, any face, it is as if curtain after curtain, mask after mask, falls away…until a final mask remains, one that can no longer be removed, reduced. By the time the drawing is finished I know a great deal about that fellow human, for no face can hide itself very long. But although nothing escapes the eye, all is forgiven beforehand. The eye does not judge, moralize, criticize. It accepts the masks in gratitude as it does the long bamboo being long, the goldenrod being yellow…

The energetic executive smile, the preacher's pious frown, the doctor's paternal smirk, the sweet-seventeen pout of the fad-ing beauty—these are the top-layer masks that vanish at the first touch of relaxation, pain, or a double martini. Each "Me" is a succession of masks. At the moment of death, with the "Me," the last mask vanishes.

Only very, very rarely have I seen a face that—fully alive, yet without mask—showed the human in all its greatness, without a trace of falsity or pretense. It was in the face of Angelo Roncalli, better known as Pope John XXIII, that I saw this pure beauty of the Spirit. He was a fat man, not handsome, but beautiful, for he was a genius of the heart...maskless.

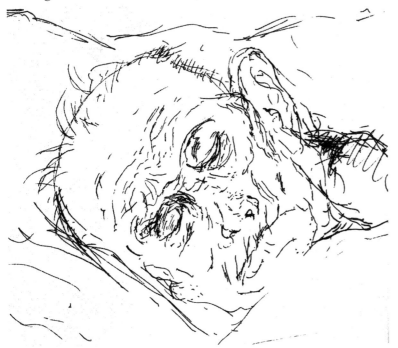

When, years ago, I first discovered Zen writings, I did not find them strange. On the contrary, they confirmed and clarified my most intimate intuitions about life. It was like discovering a strange country, and in this strange place one happened to know the roads and hills and ponds. It was home.

The Zen attitude to life is not absorbed from books, although it may be confirmed by reading. It is the inborn attitude of the True-Man-Without-Label, who may well be the artist-within...

•

On a dark afternoon—I was ten or eleven—I was walking on a country road, on my left a patch of curly kale, on my right some yellowed Brussels sprouts. I felt a snowflake on my cheek, and from far away in the charcoal-gray sky I saw the slow approach of a snow-flurry. I stood still.

Some flakes were now falling around my feet. A few melted as they hit the ground. Others stayed intact. Then I heard the falling of the snow, with the softest hissing sound. I stood transfixed in the grayness, listening...and knew what can never be expressed. Once again, the natural had become supernatural enough!

I draw a leaf...Still it is moving. Still the birds are on the wing. Still I can hear the silent falling of the snow...Some of the grasses are long, others are short...

And yet, I know artists whose medium is life itself, and who neither paint nor dance. Their medium is being. Whatever their hand touches has increased life. They SEE and don't have to draw. They are the artists of being alive.

This life is my windfall! That it happens to be a human life is the one chance in a trillion to be able to realize That Which Matters.

In seeing/drawing, that which matters can be perceived through the senses, not denied but maximally affirmed.

While seeing/drawing I glimpse into Nature, I taste Nature, the Nature of Reality: the way of seeing is a way of knowing!

•

Once, while drawing an apple tree—thinking of nothing at all, just watching, seeing, following that life story through roots, trunk, branches, twigs—the most baffling riddles solved themselves.

THE TREE BECAME HUMANITY ROOTED DEEP IN THE EARTH. ITS LIMBS WERE THE RACES, ITS TWIGS THE FAMILIES. I, WHO ONCE BELIEVED MYSELF TO BE A TREE, SAW MYSELF AS JUST ONE OF THE MYRIAD LEAVES OF ONE LONG SEASON—TO BE BLOWN AWAY A LITTLE EARLIER, A LITTLE LATER. SOME OTHER LEAVES HAD ALREADY FALLEN, MANY REMAINED STUNTED, SOME WERE STILL FRESHLY GREEN IN OCTOBER. BUT SOON THE NOVEMBER STORMS WOULD SWEEP US ALL AWAY. THEN, AFTER THE TORTURES OF FROST, THERE WOULD FOLLOW A NEW EXPLOSION OF PINK BLOSSOMS, THEN LEAVES, AND NEXT AUTUMN THE BRANCHES WOULD ONCE MORE BEND DOWN UNDER BURDENS OF FRUIT.

THE TREE HAD BECOME THE TREE OF LIFE.

CHAPTER XV

1989

FROM

Little Compendium on That Which Matters

Published by
ST. MARTIN'S PRESS

That is all too easily dismissed as "anti-intellectualism" may well be the tendency, in extremis, to reestablish some balance between thinking and feeling, between the activities of the right and left hemispheres (was perhaps the right one formerly known as "the heart"?…) after a few centuries of that heartless cerebrality which culminated in the perfect technological know-how to prepare our demise.

◆

Here it is blandly assumed that, however enigmatic, there is a Reality/Truth, a Tao, a "really-Real" which transcends the crudely empirical, that there is Meaning to our sojourn on earth and that we may even be able to grasp this Meaning or be grasped by it.
Could the Meaning of being born human be, to become Human?

◆

When logic follows experience, it is likely to be valid. When experience derives from logic, it is bound to be self-deception: delusional, spurious, false.

◆

A consensus between the religious traditions on the nature of the Transcendent/Immanent is, of course, unattainable. Nor is it indispensable. There is, however, a remarkable convergence in Christianity, Judaism, Buddhism, Sufism on the criteria of what deserves to be called "Human" and what is less than human, what is pre-human, in-human, sub-human, anti-human, even sub-animal. Where these criteria have remained all too implicit, they must at last be made clearly explicit and shouted from the housetops, as the basis of a vital transcultural, transreligious inner life, so desperately needed. The emphatic consensus on what it really means to be Human reopens the perspective, indicates the Way toward a once more livable world.

◆

Zuigan used to call out to himself:
> "Zuigan, are you there?"
> "Yes, Master!"
> "Are you wide awake?"
> "Yes, Master!"
> "Really awake?"
> "Oh, yes!"
> "And so you won't let yourself be bamboozled, confused, side-tracked again?"
> "No, Master! Never!"

◆

Anything labeled "spirituality" that is not experiential, intimately related to direct experiencing, is therefore highly suspect of being pseudo-spiritual life, self-indulgence, yet another parlor game.

Pseudo-"spirituality" is not only offered for sale, it is marketed wholesale, retail and successfully franchised. It can be ordered from dozens of mail order catalogs, or consumed on the premise, à la carte.

◆

What for the "Realpolitiker," the Naïve Realist, is "real," is sheer illusion. It denies the crucially important: the reality of every human life as an inner process between birth and death. It is their rash little dance on the thin ice that covers the precipice of Nothingness.

◆

"People make faces as if they were going to live forever" says *an ancient Japanese senryu.*

◆

The collision of the empirical ego in its delusions with the unyielding iceberg of the Real is the inescapable moment of Truth in every human life. It leaves us with two options: either to awaken to the Reality of the human condition, and proceed toward ultimate integration, or to flounder toward terminal disintegration. When all technological devices have failed, all escape hatches are closed, the moment of *metanoia* may be at hand.

◆

Ego, ("I am, you aren't, they aren't") the concommittant of *avidya,* primordial ignorance, in Buddhism (and perhaps of the Fall in Judeo-Christianity), is by nature ruthless, violent. The collective or in-group ego is just as intrinsically massmurderous.

◆

Ego looks, looks out for itself, but is blind as a bat. When I SEE I am all eye; ego is momentarily forgotten, I am nothing but a focus of awareness. "The Meaning of Life is to See," said Hui Neng, and another master: "I am not worried about what you do, how you conduct your life, for I approve of how you *see*."

◆

Hui Hai, 9th century, says: "Your treasure house is within you, it contains all you'll ever need..." and Thomas's Gospel: "The Kingdom is within you and around you."

◆

To be aware of still breathing (until it stops), of the earth (as long as it lasts), of feeling hungry and delighted with a fresh egg, a piece of still-warm bread, is to be still part of humanity.

◆

"Belief" is one of the expressions of faith. But, it implies assent to dogmatic propositions on someone else's authority. Beliefs therefore may be a hurdle to "pure experience," to intuitive perception of Reality/Truth. Mark Twain's schoolboy who interpreted: "Faith is to believe what you know ain't so!" confused faith with belief.

◆

Faith is a Specifically Human constituent while "beliefs" are the forms it assumes at certain stages of spiritual maturation. Beliefs are time- and culture-bound.

◆

On the exoteric level the religious traditions are therefore irreconcilable. On the esoteric, experiential level of the heart reigns an eloquent, reverential silence.

◆

Contempt of and animosity toward "the others" is so ingrained, that we have the greatest difficulty taking their view of life seriously. Indoctrination is so persuasive that we can't help assuming that "they" too are programmed, be it incorrectly.

◆

As long as the non-Christian religions are considered as mere antipasto for the Last Supper, all ecumenism is fraudulent.

◆

When Hui Hai was asked: "Are Buddhism, Taoism and Confucianism three different religions or one and the same?" he answered:

"For men of the highest capacity they are one. For the mediocre they are three. For those below this level they are not only three, but irreconcilable... Whether a man reaches liberation, however, depends on himself, not on differences in doctrine."

◆

About Eckhart's Godhead, about the Void, the Dharmakaya, Sunyata, I can mumble without feeling either fool or hypocrite. If I talk about a conventional personal God, an updated Yahweh, I hear myself sound phony: This word "God" is all too superannuated, too thoroughly polluted by too many scoundrels...

◆

Still, when I speak to God—at times one can't help oneself—He/She is Absolutely Personal.

◆

The French philosopher Simone Weil could say: "God is both personal and impersonal, and neither."

◆

We have been immensely enriched, spiritually revitalized by the mystical traditions and insights of Asia, by the rehabilitation of what Leibniz, and after him Aldous Huxley, called "the perennial philosophy." What is heresy to the goose, may be spiritual rebirth to the gander.

◆

It is not the self-deprecating "I am nothing" that sets me free, but the insight that "NoThingness is Me": that I am a fleeting condensation of this NoThing, this really-Real that is unchanging in its pattern of uninterrupted change.

◆

"Zen" may be that which in the religious traditions is the truly essentially "religious" perception that is trans-religious and even trans-cultural.

◆

The all too real heresy of our time is that alienation from the profundity of human life, of which the advance guard is that Scientism/Technology which, ignoring Reality/Truth, takes all that transcends, that defies objectification as objectifiable and even quantifiable. Oddly, its rear guard is that fundamentalism which recycles scriptural clichés as the solution to all existential riddles, that objectifies the Ultimately Unobjectifiable into a sacrosanct Thing.

◆

The opposite of faith as an openness to Reality/Truth is neither unbelief, skepticism nor doubt. It is the un-faith, the anti-faith that characterizes the deadly syndrome of Nihilism.

◆

Modern Nihilism is that highly structured anti-faith, which like a submarine earthquake has undermined all spiritual values as well as all the classical humanistic ones: veracity, fair play, constancy, tolerance, compassion, generosity—including honor and noblesse. It destroys the roots, it poisons the wells, it subverts the ground on which human life, culture, community are possible.

◆

Victorious in the West, Nihilism is colonizing, "globalizing," by corporate conspiracy that is Westernizing the Third World, uprooting autochthonic traditions and cultures, destroying the ties of peoples to their earth, their traditional, agricultural and economic systems. It reduces entire populations to the condition of a permanent sub-proletariat, enslaved to multinational power machinery.

◆

Millions of people are tortured, killed, deported, kidnapped, enslaved, starved. Numberless children are dying today, while we prattle of peace…

◆

"Peace is not an absence of war," Spinoza said, but it is mindlessly quoted out of context, for he added, "it is a virtue, a state of mind, a disposition for benevolence, confidence, justice."

◆

What one is likely to lose sight of is that during one's existence-time, I—as all things and beings—am never anything of a temporary "condensation" of this Absolute No-Thingness, this Primal Mystery. Yet, it is during this brief span of existence, of time, that I must live the timeless—that is: "eternity." Mere condensation that I am, I am no phantom, I am real, and have the capacity to watch the entire, eternal cosmic drama of the formless condensing itself into form, yet remaining itself.

◆

The micro-moment of awareness that my eye truly meets your eye, that the "condensation" of Nothingness which I call "Me" embraces that condensation I call "You," is the moment of Truth, of the oneness of Life, beyond love, beyond friendship, beyond all self-labeling as being a "This" or a "That."

◆

Could it be that the swift alternation, each day, of overwhelming beauty and tenderness with unspeakable cruelty, stupidity, horror and evil is the only spiritual discipline we need—provided all the senses are kept open, no moodlifters taken—to awaken to the great Guru, the Master at our core?

Yes!

THE "SOCIAL MASK" OPENED TO
LAY BARE THE TRUE SELF

CHAPTER XVI

1994

FROM

Fingers Pointing Toward the Sacred

Published by

BEACON POINT PRESS

Contemporary human. Human without fixed abode. No longer does he/she live in an environment, exists in a context, a context that is ceaselessly shifting, nationally, culturally, religiously, ecologically, politically. Here I am, flying in a context, shifting at the speed of sound. A mere specimen of contemporary man am I, homeless adventurer against his will, involuntary globetrotter, whose travel agent is the nightmare-idol we call History, chased from our home ground by economic disaster, by political or racial persecution, by war and rumors of war, partitions, revolutions. Even if, for the moment of being, we escape these involuntary wanderings we are driven to fly all over the globe as tourist, businessman, executive, researcher, salesman, spy, do-gooder, terrorist.

If compelled to stay put, we instantly are turned into vicarious globetrotters, daily uprooted by radio, television, and newspaper to be immersed in the conflicts, the violence, the horrors, the ideas and ideologies, the fads, the religions, the superstitions, and pseudo-religions of all seven continents. Mobility, no longer purely geographical and social, has become uncontrollable mobility into the onrushing future of ever-accelerated change that does not change a wit what matters.

In response to our ever-shifting context, our shifting "Me" seems to form itself, a "Me" constantly changing, adapting itself by chains of action-reaction to the un-catalogued, unclassifiable, infinite chaos of cultural, technological, artificial political stimuli, influences, and conventions. This "Me" contains our whole unsteady lexicon of notions about world, nature, man,

God, Christ, nation, race, self, no-self.

Narada Mahathera, in his seventies, is one of the most distinguished Buddhist scholars of Sri Lanka. When I first met him in his threadbare saffron-yellow habit, I took him for a working monk in the monastery of which he is the abbot. His manner is as unassuming as his appearance, but he radiates quiet authority.

"Buddhism as well as Christianity is based on fear," he explains, "on fear of the unknown. Buddhism is homocentric, Christianity is theocentric. Buddhism is introverted, Christianity is extroverted."

"To me Christo-centricity is at the same time homocentric and theocentric," I interject. "Christology is an anthropology, just as Buddhology is an anthropology," I hear myself assert. "Both deal with the deepest, truest, essential nature of man. Both Christ and Buddha are to me the living, incarnate criteria of what it really means to be human. Does this sound unacceptable to you?"

He cocks an eyebrow and gestures for me to continue.

"As far as Buddhism's introversion is concerned, by itself I find that of no merit. If it is not balanced by extroversion toward the world, it leaves the world in its mess. If humans are worthy of being enlightened, they are worthy of being fed! Buddhism seems to be lacking a compelling social ethic; has often been seen as all too unconcerned with social justice, with the needs of concrete human beings. What you call Christian extroversion on the other hand, has indeed the tendency to become a meddlesome paternalistic activism, unaware of the need for a profound self-examination—I mean examination of what Self really is—and so it makes the world's mess even messier. Do you see any chance of integration of Christian and Buddhist values and meanings, Narada Mahathera? Could not Eastern introversion and Western activism complement one another? Isn't it high time for a synthesis?"

"The differences are too fundamental! Better leave Christianity Christianity and Buddhism Buddhism! First there is your Judeo-Christian God. When I was once lecturing in a church in London I was asked about our Buddhist denial of God. I answered, 'How can I, sitting under the very roof of God, have the discourtesy to deny him?' But as you know, we reject the idea of a personal God who created the world *ex nihilo* and demands to be feared and obeyed. The exclusive sonship of Christ makes no sense to us at all, neither his role as Savior of an immortal soul. First of all, we do not believe man has an immortal ego-soul.

"The Buddha does not pretend to be a savior. He is the teacher who exhorts his disciples to depend on themselves in order to reach liberation. He does not condemn men by calling them wretched sinners, but he gladdens them by showing that they are potentially pure in heart."

"Isn't there here a parallel to the Christian 'glad tidings'?" I asked. "Jesus shows in his words and especially in his manner of life and death, his fullest acceptance of what you call karma. He demonstrates the full potentiality of man, the kingdom that is within."

"Christ is a Savior," he insisted vehemently. "To believe in him is to achieve salvation. Nobody is saved by believing in the Buddha. A man is saved by following his teachings, by living the Dharma, by living according to the law of reality, of the truth. Buddhism does not deal in superstitious rites and ceremonies, dogmas, sacrifices, and "repentance" as the price of salvation. Repentance is simply the will not to repeat one's foolishness. The teaching of Buddha, the Dharma, is grounded in factual reality. Buddhism is a philosophical and ethical system which our human experience can verify as being in accord with reality. It neither violates conscience nor intelligence. It leaves thought free, is without fanaticism, and does not know persecution."

I tried, "Many contemporary Christians would not object to a formulation that would run approximately: God is the very ground of my Being. God equals the ultimate reality. If I may use my own private language: God is the very Structure of Reality. I see the Christ as the one who discerns the Structure of Reality, recognizes it within himself as his ground, as his deepest self, and who empties himself of the delusional ego."

"Buddhism denies the reality of the ego. There is no *atman*, no self," Narada said severely.

"That is not the whole of Buddhism, is it?" I objected. "That is Theravada. Mahayana does not see the self as mere illusion. The 'True Self,' according to this view, is the empirical psychological self, but minus its egocentric, narcissistic delusions. The 'True Self,' after this discounting of ego, is as rich in content as ever before, even immensely richer, because it no longer stands pitted against the world but contains the world within itself. *Anatta* (the 'absence of *atman*') according to this view, means that there is no psychological substratum corresponding to the word self. May I continue? Christ lives his identification with his Ground, with the Structure of Reality to the point where he can call it Father. 'I and the Father are one, not two.' He manifests this supreme insight in his compassionate love, his agape that he pours impartially on the just and the unjust."

"You give an extremely Buddhist interpretation of Christianity. Or a Christian interpretation of Buddhism! You would have trouble selling it at All Saints!"

"I can't sit cross-legged and I feel I don't have to. It would be unnatural for me, unnecessary," I said.

"It isn't absolutely necessary. So what is your way?"

"My way is simply to see. When I see an ox and I draw that ox, I become this ox and I see, I realize its oxness, the mystery of its creatureliness, of impermanence in it and in me. We become equivalent in our condition of creatureliness. While I am drawing a hunchback or an old woman, they become at least as beautiful for me as an athlete or a beauty queen. When I draw a tree or the children on their ponies in the sunset on the beach, I see them in their transiency. I see that conditioning can create fresh karma. Karma therefore has a certain plasticity. It can be transformed by insight and praxis... According to Theravada Buddhism there is no God, no allover purpose in the universe, no 'creation,' just a cyclic ebb and flood of universes. A human being, any sentient being, is a series of connected psychosomatic events, point-moments, governed by karmic law."

"Karmic law cannot be proven, can it? In that respect it is very much like God's providence, divine justice."

"It is a point of faith, but also of observation," Narada said a bit sourly.

"Could you say something about the idea of transcendence in Theravada Buddhism?"

There is Nibbana (Nirvana). The Udana sutra says: 'There is a not-born, not-become, not-created, not-formed. If there were not this not-born, not-become, not-created, not-formed, then an escape from the born, the become, the created, the formed could not be known...'" This and the Heart Sutra stress the Structure of Reality for me.

When on that October day in 1962 I heard John XXIII make his opening speech to the Second Vatican Council he had called, it was like hearing the ringing of the bells on Easter morning and the rising of the meadowlark. "It is only dawn," the old pope had exclaimed at the height of the Cuban missile crisis. He was obviously more than just a pope, this Enlightened One, who happened to be pope. I, who am religiously unaffiliated, felt his Council was going to be the crucial spiritual event of my lifetime. I flew to Rome to do hundreds of drawings of the drama and its star actors during Vatican II's four sessions. I shared the euphoria when Angelo Roncalli threw the windows open, and the despondence when he died and they were being

pushed shut once more. Vatican II became indeed a watershed, if not the way anyone, except perhaps the Spirit, had planned it.

Again I stood in the Piazza San Pietro, on the very spot where on that sunny Thursday, December 8, 1962 I had been sketching what the newspapers used to call "the purple waterfall" of three thousand cardinals and bishops walking, shuffling, limping down the steps of St. Peter's at the end of the daily session to their waiting limousines and buses. That day all lingered in the piazza, for Pope John was going to speak. The window opened, and there, with the cancer inside gnawing him away, stood Angelo Roncalli smiling and waving, spreading out his arms as if to embrace the whole world. His still strong voice came over the loudspeakers, "Slowly, slowly I am coming up. Sickness, then convalescence! What a spectacle before me today! The whole church standing here together!"

And then he started to sing. Of course he knew, as we all did, that he was dying. But the vigorous gravelly Italian voice sang as if there were no death.

This was the man I saw as the greatest, the most human of my life-time, a Christian Boddhisattva! First pope in the two millennia long procession of power-hungry popes, who dared to answer a question with: "How could I know! I am only the pope!"

He is the pope who threw open the windows of his Church, let fresh air blow in, let the cobwebs and dust balls whirl over red plush thrones and guilded inlaid consoles. The entire exquisite interior was in intolerable disarray. But then...Pope John died. And at once hundreds of prelates slaved day and night to push cobwebs and dust balls back into the corners where they belonged until, at last, the place was beginning to look respectable again. Nevertheless, almost forty years later Pope John and his message are as alive as ever, even survived his canonization together with one of his most reactionary predecessors. It was obviously a practical joke of high Vatican diplomacy...

DHARAMSALA

"The Tourist Hotel"—a dirty yellow cube—"very posh, very clean, good food," the doctor in the bus had assured me, stands close to the bus stop. Under a bare bulb, a faded sign reads: "Modern rooms. Private baths. Oriental and Western cuisine."

The dark taproom smells of sweat. On half of the tables lamps with tiny bulbs create atmosphere. The phonograph sounds as an asthmatic sea lion. A couple of forlorn lovers hold hands in the gloom. The elderly owner in shirtsleeves and citron-yellow turban, bows like a maitre d'hotel at Maxim's. We sit down on a rickety bench in one of the booths, drink tea from dirty cups.

There is a telephone. I call the Government Rest House, no answer, the Tourist Bungalow, no vacancy. With another elegant bow, the owner presents a greasy menu.

"Our staff is on vacation," he says, "but I could make you parathas. I also have some cold mutton on toast."

He puts the guestbook in front of me on the grimy table. I glance at my predecessor in misfortune, and read: Beethoven, Ludwig van, mechanic, U.S.A., date of arrival 12/5/1978, date of departure 8/9/1840. Address: YU8-7432.

"Is this correct?" I ask, showing him my entry.

"Sorry, Sah, I can't read."

Our room has wooden bedsteads, covered with eiderdowns black with years of grime. Underneath the comforters there is no mattress. A wooden bottom of planks is stamped "This side up."

"Is there no bedding?"

"Guests usually bring their own, Sah. I think I have two sheets, but they cost extra."

"And towels, please!" He returns with a tiny pink towel decorated with the word Hers.

The climate is bracing, around 15 degrees. We sit on a newspaper spread over the comforters and read the Hsin-hsin Ming:

"There is no here, no there. Infinity is before our eyes. The infinitely large is as small as the infinitely minute. If one wishes to turn to the One Vehicle, one must have no aversion to the objects of the senses."

It is a fifteen-minute climb from the village to the Dalai Lama's compound. Old Tibetan women, bent under loads of firewood, fold their hands in greeting, children hold their hands together in front of their chest, smile and bow. Patriarchal old men in fur caps with earflaps, turning a prayer wheel, immersed in prayer, pass me chanting. Over the great valley, large white birds circle in clear, thin air. At the gate of the compound armed Indian guards check passports, telephone the Dalai Lama's secretary, Lama Tenzing Geiche, who has been expecting us since yesterday. In the drawing room, where holy books wrapped in orange and blue cloth fill the shelves of glassed bookcases, we talk about Sri Lanka and Hinayana Buddhism, about Africa and Schweitzer.

"By the way, where are you staying?" He knows all about the Tourist Hotel.

"We can accommodate you in the guest cottage of His Holiness, but it is a steep thirty minute climb, do you mind? His Holiness will make time for you in a few days. We'll be in touch."

Our path leads past the barbed-wire fence that surrounds the compound. An Indian soldier, rifle at his side, stands dozing in front of his sentry box, another sentry has made a fire and is cooking lunch. The trail, part path, part rock-hewn staircase, winds along the edge of a steep precipice. From bushes and trees wave faded gauze prayer flags. Every few yards people have built stone heaps, symbolical mandalas, from two to five feet high. On a large bare rock the words OM MANI PADME HUM—"Om, the jewel in the Lotus"—have been carved in large Tibetan script, filled in with red, white, yellow, blue, and green paint. At the cottage, on the wide terrace overlooking the splendid immensity of valley, the housekeeper awaits us with her little daughter. We have a whole suite to ourselves! There is a cozy sitting room, logs are burn-

ing in the fireplace, a clean bedroom with a stone floor, a bathroom, even a water heater! A maid with a lovely flat Tibetan moon face, quietly puts tea and biscuits in front of the fire. Dawa Chodon speaks a little English.

"Please rest," she says, "you must be hungry. Lunch will be ready soon."

I take Claske by the shoulders. Was last night a dream? Is this a dream?

And I repeat the words of Shah Jahan on the Red Fort in Delhi, "If paradise be on the face of the earth, this is it, this is it, this is it!"

Visit with Dalai Lama (1972)

In the early afternoon the Indian guards at the gate of the official compound copy our passports. We are frisked, have to leave matches, pen knife, even a nail file.

His Holiness, the fourteenth Dalai Lama, Sakya Gejong Tenzin Gyatsho, is tall, surprisingly youthful, with a smile that is exceptionally radiant, even for a Tibetan. He shakes hands informally and points at a modern Swedish settee opposite him. His room is bright and comfortable, the furniture simple and modern. Although his English is surprisingly excellent, Tenzing Geiche helps out with a word here and there. When a young lama comes in with coffee, I have to move over and sit next to the Dalai Lama. He keeps replenishing my cup from a silver coffeepot. Tenzing Geiche has obviously briefed him. He wants to hear all about my trans-religious "Pacem in

Gal Vihara, Polonnaruwa, Ceylon '71   Luciano Francis

BUDDHAS — SRI LANKA

Terris" sanctuary in Warwick, N.Y., and what it has taught me about the spiritual life of the young.

"I too have met very many young people in these last eleven years of exile. I have come to see that cultural and age gaps are almost always spiritual gaps. The young, the hippies? They come in dozens to Dharamsala. What does it matter that they look unkempt? They express the hopelessness of people when their traditional cultural ideals suddenly reveal themselves as being empty of meaning. Long hair does not stand in the way of the search for ultimate meaning, neither does a shaven head help it," he smiles, rubbing his own.

"Of course, Buddhism must have an enormous attraction for people, when the sponginess, the hollowness of power, the unreliability of money, of status, all the doubtful benefits of 'progress' dawn upon them. It must be a revelation then to find a religion which sees the 'Jewel in the Lotus,' the Buddha-nature, not only in every human being, but even in every sentient being, a religion that gives a supreme meaning and vocation, an infinite dignity to every human life, and which puts the responsibility for attaining the supreme insight squarely on one's own shoulders and stimulates us to reach it by our own efforts. The good qualities in humanity are our only hope. This doesn't mean at all that the bad ones are overlooked or ignored, but that the basic quality that tends to be good and noble must be recognized, emphasized, cultivated, encouraged. Where else lies hope?"

He has been told of my work with Albert Schweitzer.

"I have been fascinated with Dr. Schweitzer from the time I was a little boy. Tell me, tell me."

For an hour or so I reminisce about my work with the "Grand Docteur" at the hospital at Lambaréné, but he keeps asking me questions.

"What is your final evaluation of Albert Schweitzer?"

"He was one of the three men in my life who has given me most. Schweitzer was a very great human being, almost over life-size, and a pioneer. As a doctor, as early as 1913, he was a pioneer in true foreign aid to the needy, without any political or religious strings attached. As a theologian he was a pioneer in a new approach to biblical research. As a musician he was responsible for one of the few things that do honor to our time: the rediscovery of Johann Sebastian Bach. At age 86 he was still a pioneer, this time in his protest against atom-bomb testing. He was also a pioneer in missionary work, placing service above the obsession with nominal conversion. He was a pioneer in practical ecumenism. As a doctor, musician, philosopher he pushed every one of his potentialities to its furthest limits. What more may one expect from a man?"

"How about his 'Reverence for Life'?"

"It was a noble inspiration. He gave me a photograph of the spot on the Ogowe River where in 1915 it came to him as a transcendental experience, an illumination. Still, to me, 'I have reverence for life' is an amazing statement. What is that 'I' that has reverence for life? As if there were a dichotomy between 'I' and 'life!' As if 'I' were anything but 'life!' One step further and he would have broken through the barrier of ego and he would be my third Bodhisattva. Now I honor his memory as that of a great man, a great personality with whom I was privileged to work, a noble ego."

"You have just touched on something very crucial, on the split between 'I' and 'the other,' between 'I' and 'life itself.' In this all schools of Buddhism (as it is called in the West; we prefer the traditional term Dharma) agree. The quintessence of Dharma is that one understands the causes in oneself of one's own *dukkha,* or pain, thereby becoming able to tell others of these causes. Precisely your question 'Who is this "I" who has reverence?' is indeed solved in Buddhist thought, which says, 'To suppose that things and beings exist independently, have an ego-nature, is the "atman-view" and this is still ignorance.' For one who is freed, this ego-view is destroyed. It is the highest aspect of insight. This does not mean that the sense objects perceived by the five senses are negated, but that our conventional, relativistic view of them is seen as being incomplete. The living person who goes on from day to day is real enough, but the innate Me-feeling of all beings has at most a relative reality. One of the virtues of a Buddha is that he lets the rain of his friendliness and compassion fall steadily and continuously upon all suffering beings."

"I believe, Your Holiness, that what you have just expressed is the neglected essence of Christianity as well as Buddhism."

The Christian mystic, Tauler, has said, "Nothing burns in hell but the ego." One could paraphrase this, "Nothing is crucified but ego; nothing is resurrected but Christ!"

"Who are the other two men who meant so much to you?"

"The others are Pope John and Daisetz Teitaro Suzuki. All three were over eighty when I met them, all three had a spirit that was eternally young. Pope John is the one I love the most, for he was all warmth and humanness. I see him as a genius of the heart, as a Catholic Bodhisattva, who far transcended being a pope. In his last years I believe he was truly enlightened, his ego had dissolved. Not a trace of narcissism was left. Whatever he did came from the Self. 'I am only the pope,' he would say. He had overcome all prejudices. He had overcome the theology of the scribes, which has estranged us from the Light that enlightens every individual who comes into the world. Having overcome his own ego, the Church as collective in-group ego did not worry him very much. Speaking of his own impending death he said: 'My bags are packed.' His humor, his tolerance, freedom, compassion, his wisdom, his intrepidity, all were integrated. To me he was proof that enlightenment can be reached through any spiritual discipline, in his case a very conventional Catholic one. To put it in Christian terms I see him as a manifestation of the Holy Spirit."

The Dalai Lama smiled his assent and asked, "And Suzuki?"

"I came upon his writings about thirty years ago as upon a revelation, and he has remained my almost daily companion. He is one of those rare human beings who is able to express the inexpressible and transmit the intransmissible from many

SILENTIUM.

Frederick Franck

different angles, so that it may penetrate on many levels of the reader's awareness and make multiple living connections with his reader's own insights. He never leads one astray into bogus mysticism or esoteric symbolism; on the contrary, he cuts off all evasions, self-indulgences, rationalizations, and conceptualizations, in order to point directly at the self-nature, that Buddha Nature that we do not 'have' but are, beyond the empirical ego. Suzuki attempts to lead his reader to the great wisdom-compassion, to 'a realization which is not self-realization, but realization pure and simple, beyond subject and object,' as Thomas Merton expressed it.

"To my mind Suzuki too was a Bodhisattva, one who attained full enlightenment, then dwelt among those who search and suffer in order to offer them a glimpse of reality, of enlightenment. Neither he nor Pope John had a doctrine to teach, these men were the very doctrine they taught."

"Did you ever meet Suzuki?"

"In 1955 I visited him. I wondered if what I had gleaned from his books had any validity at all, or was it all nonsense? I had written down my thoughts to save him time, to impose as little as possible on him."

"What did he say?"

"He just gave me a radiant smile and said, 'It is not nonsense.'"

"I have noticed so often that if people dare to reveal their innermost concerns, their reality, if they speak from heart to heart, there is perfect understanding. All barriers fall away and communication is so easy."

"Your Holiness, I am amazed to feel at this moment not as if I were drinking coffee with…the Dalai Lama, but simply with a fellow human being. It makes me extremely happy and it gives me the courage to ask you, "Do you think it would be a useful experiment to X-ray, as it were, Christian concepts or rather insights, by means of Buddhist ones and vice versa? In this time of confusion and barbarism I can't think of anything that could be more important than the clarification of and reorientation toward the deepest existential insights the human spirit has achieved and which are hidden in the religions. I realize that it would be a huge task, a collective one. I have not the slightest illusion as to my personal competence. But I am convinced in my very heart that such equivalents exist and that they are the key to a reorientation to what it means to be human."

The Dalai Lama said, "I believe not only that it is useful and think it is possible, but that in the present state of the world nothing indeed could be more important. A flawless understanding among the religions is not an impossible ideal. The followers of each religion should understand as much as possible of the religions of others precisely because in their deepest aspirations all religions, whatever their differences, point toward the same reality, the reality that lies at the root of every human being. You have my blessings!"

"I am very grateful," I said, "but, excuse me if this sounds terribly rude, I always have difficulty with that word 'blessing'!

It confuses me. Isn't it more or less your profession to bestow blessings? During the Vatican Council I drew all those bishops and cardinals and they were always blessing. I often asked myself, 'What on earth does it mean?' After all, it is even less expensive for popes and patriarchs to bless than for kings to give away titles and medals!"

He found this amusing and laughed aloud, "What is your solution to the riddle?" "Could a real blessing be that, knowing of one's own fullness of heart, one lets it overflow?"

"It might be giving, by knowing of the other's need. It is *upaya* (stratagem, skillful means). By the way, do you feel a little at home here, are you comfortable at the cottage?"

"Strange as it may seem, we feel completely at home. We come from the other side of the earth, don't speak a word of Tibetan, and after a week it feels as if we have lived here forever. We fell in love at first sight with your people."

"Maybe it is because you don't speak a word of Tibetan," he quipped.

Then he said gravely, "My people have lost everything, their country, their families, their homes, and they carry on. They are innocent people."

He spoke about the hardships of the refugees, their hardships in social and climatic readjustment, then he came back to the inner revolution among many of the young in the West.

"Is it really a revolution?" he wondered.

"I don't think revolution is really the right word. Maybe it is a mutation in awareness, which is something that takes place on a deeper level. It is the search of those who are no longer obsessed with technological utopias, but with the meaning of human life."

He said something in Tibetan to Tenzing Geiche, who disappeared and came back with the Dalai Lama's book *The Opening of the Wisdom Eye.* "This is quite elementary," he said, "but I also want to give you this."

It was a thin volume on Tantric meditation. Again he said something in Tibetan. Tenzing Geiche translated, "This book is given to very few people, whom His Holiness feels have a sincere and serious understanding of Buddhism."

The fourteenth Dalai Lama, Sakya Gejong Tenzin Gyatsho, then repeated it in English, took my hands and we both held the book. He also gave us a fine painted Tibetan *thanka* scroll.

•

As we left the modest palace and the dusk was blotting out the immense valley, a procession emerged from the Thekchen Choling, the Tibetan "cathedral." Lamas in ox-blood red, pleated cloaks and cadmium yellow tricornered hats strode down the steps, preceded by an old abbot leaning on a staff, a yellow scarf over his deep red cloak. Young lamas blew silver shawms. Others carried sixteen-foot-long silver horns, the drums, cymbals, and bells and a large red stupa-shape, sculptured in butter. The procession moved solemnly down the narrow path to the entrance of the village, where a tepee-shaped structure had been built of branches and leaves, then came to a halt. A young monk in a bright yellow and blue cloth apron and a white gauze scarf over his cloak brought offerings of water and apples. The chanting and the tellurian groans of the huge horns, accompanied by the shrill voices of the shawms, filled the thin mountain air. Old men and women prayed aloud, twirling cylindrical prayer wheels. It was nearly dark when the butter sculpture was placed inside the hut, which was then ignited. Flames shot up high into the deep-turquoise sky, consuming all the evil spirits and the worries of the past year. The New Year had started. In the blackness we stumbled down the steep path to the guesthouse.

•

That so many now turn East in search of a spiritual shelter in our wasteland is neither mere fashion nor fad. We, late 20th-century people, who have ham and eggs for breakfast, sushi for lunch and Madras curry for supper, are no longer living in walled-in cultural ghettos, where beliefs are locked in fixed pre-suppositions and actions that are shared by all. We are not like the ancient Hebrews for whom Yahweh, as the icon of the divine, was part of the tribal cultural system, hence far beyond even a thought of doubt, let alone rejection. If not politically and ethnically, at any rate gastronomically and spiritually the world is fast becoming a single continent. We find our home where the heart feels at ease. Convergences, isomorphisms, parallelisms in religious experience have become inevitable. A new image of the Specifically Human, the Humanum, may be hovering over the maelstrom of contem-

MAHAKASYAPA

porary nihilism and cynicism. Hence I never became a card-carrying Buddhist just as I never became a Catholic, or even a "Christian."

I can't help being a loner, incurably allergic to joining anything whatsoever, whether political party, church, sect, cult or even Zen center. I must have suspected at quite a tender age that as far as the need for "identity" is concerned, my (and everyone else's) only real, colorfast, identity is simply to be Human, to recognize that "Original Face one had before even one's parents were born." I shivered at the very thought of being caught up in one of those nets of "identities" that pit groups of humans against one another.

I felt the Bodhisattva concept of Mahayana—the Enlightened One who in his wisdom/compassion foregoes the beatitude of Nirvana until all beings are saved or awakened—to be totally compatible with the Judaic "Just" for whom the world is to be spared and with the *Jivanmukta* of Hinduism.

The *Jivanmukta* transcends scriptures and conventions, even ethical codes, but cannot do anything that is not conducive to the well-being of others. The Bodhisattva wears no outer mask of holiness, enjoys life, but never forgets the divine Self, the presence of Brahman. He has reached highest insight.

Jivanmukta, Bodhisattva, and the Just were the ones who have attained the fullness of their humanness—call it *Imago Dei,* call it Humanum, call it *kokoro.*

The man on the cross who died and rose, had manifested millennia ago the supreme paradigm of this fully Human man-ifestation of our own potential of specific, "absolute" Humanness.

Mahayana Buddhism sees it as our "primal" or "original," our *Ur-Natur,* our Buddha Nature. Hui Neng's "Original Face," is what the Christian mystic Nicholas of Cusa spoke of as "The Face of faces discernible in all faces, veiled as in a riddle…"

What the gospel of St. John proclaims to be the "Light that lightens every human being come into the world" must be this divine spark, this True Self that lies fathoms deep beyond Little Me, the empirical ego.

The precondition for even glimpsing this Light is, in all the traditions: insight into the delusional aspects of ego. It is the Origin, Lodestar and, at the same time, culmination point of the inner human journey. It is That Which Matters, under whatever name, whether in East or in West. It is that which transcends The Naked Ape, The Anthropoid, in us: it is our human specificity!

It never occurred to me, however, that one had to "believe" something or other. One merely had to *see,* to experience it. The symbols were there! They needed no "explanation," no commentary. They were translinear and through them the Invisible Structure of Reality became perceptible. All by themselves they changed one's vision of the world, transilluminated it. Any "explanations," exegesis could only distort this direct, "poetic," perception.

Western poetic, aesthetic metaphors, its works of great, that is—authentic—art, Bach's St. Matthew's Passion,

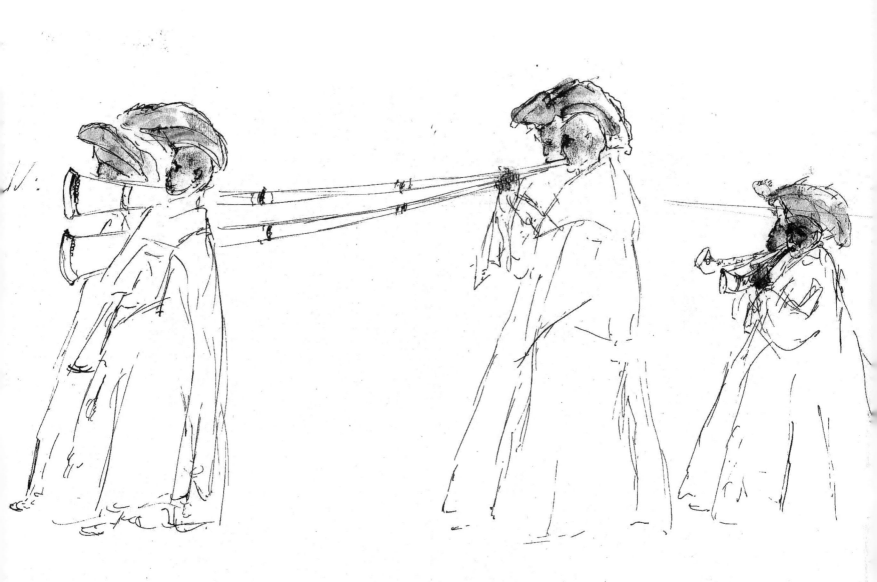

TIBETAN LAMAS WITH HUGE HORNS

Michelangelo's Pieta, Rembrandt's Emmaus, Piero della Francesca's icons, the great Western myths of Burning Bush, of Immaculate Conception, of Crucifixion and Resurrection, are of abyssal profundity, and no less self-validating, no less relevant to our own spiritual life as those of the East. The myth of the Buddha's birth, in which newly born from his mother's side, Siddharta "took seven steps, pointed one hand to Heaven, the other to Earth and proclaimed: I am born to be enlightened for the well-being of the world" is of marvelous beauty; so is that of the Immaculate Conception for those who can read it.

The great myths resonate in us, illuminate the mysteries of human life that are unattainable to the intellect.

To "explain" a myth, to "demythologize" it, is to pronounce it dead, in order to justify performing a postmortem on it. For one for whom the myth is still alive, not yet filed under "mythology," such an autopsy amounts to wanton vivisection, as heartless as it is sacrilegious. The great myths, East or West, yield their living secrets, their Wisdom heart to heart.

Awed and moved by St. John's Prologue and later by Upanishads, Heart Sutra, Fa T'Sang's Hua Yen, by Hui Neng, Rinzai, and Meister Eckhart, I found these not to contradict one another but to transilluminate each other: all speak of the Inexpressible That Matters.

There were no jarring dissonants in the essence of being Human they all revealed, each in its own way. They affirmed what I vaguely knew to be hidden somewhere in myself, however far removed I might still be from touching it.

Where "For Sale" signs and billboards cover the landscape, it is knocked soulless, the earth is desecrated. No wonder we speak of it as "dirt!" "Dirt" can be bought, haggled over, covered with mean developments, choked by condos and shopping malls. "Dirt" can be bullied at will, bulldozed, landscaped, eroded, poisoned and debased into toxic landfills, peddled as real estate, that is neither estate nor real.

Climbing that mountain trail near Dharamsala, wondering how on earth I could feel so naturally, so viscerally, at home on this steep Himalayan path, I suddenly became aware of all those little stupas that were peering out of the grass, and the rock with Om Mani Padme Hum carved in Tibetan characters—they were fingers pointing home, fingers pointing toward the Sacred!

In Japan too I had at once this intimate "at home" feeling, for the familiar jam jars full of poppies, daisies and violets stood around little Shinto shrines everywhere, not only in villages but even a hundred yards from my hotel near Tokyo station.

CHAPTER XVII

2002

FROM

Seeing Venice:
An Eye in Love

Published by

CODHILL PRESS

There are a 1001 books on Venice, from the deluxe coffeetable photo-rhapsodies via the highbrow cultural and historic tomes to the low-brow little guides for the one-day sightseer armed with camera and camcorder

This book, however, is dedicated to those whose senses are not yet numbed, whose eye is not dulled by saturation with constant electronic imagery; to anyone in whom the artist-within survived all conditioning, and hence first-hand seeing still takes precedence over looking-at, un-addicted to purblind clicking of shutters.

In this book, drawings and words are not separate categories, but form a single process: Venice is so much more than canals, bridges, gondolas. It is an unbroken sequence of ever-changing moods, festive, frivolous, elegiac and melancholy, forever foreign yet totally intimate. I retrieve here, unscathed, the visions of my Dutch childhood in the vastness of the Lagoon where round-nosed barges are still plying, swift sailboats and every kind of craft cleave the grisaille opalescences of cumulus, the diaphonous veils of vapour.

I did not "design" this book. It grew out of this process, quite riddle-some as it is. For it is a mystery, this image-making passion in which a surplus of wonder, of awe, seems to activate the hand to leave tracings on paper when the light strikes the fleeting forms of water, cloud, palazzo, human face, to fuse in lines and dots and words into a single living fabric, trusting that somehow, a kindred eye may resuscitate these traces of pure experiencing in which the "Ten thousand Things and I reveal themselves as being of one root," as an ancient Chinese put it.

The process did not start at once on my first visit to Venice. I was overwhelmed by it. Venice became at once a fascinating object, while I

Bersaglieri Carnevale '82
15/II 82

remained the subject. Quite soon, however, subject and object fused, no longer separated from one another, when I started to draw that pillared, domed, scrolled, waterlogged dream-land. Venice started to project itself on my paper in lines, dots and words, this one city on earth protected by God and/or a lagoon from invasion by car, bus and truck, so that the only way to get around - apart from brief runs on the decks of vaporettos - is on foot.

I no longer looked-at Venice, I saw it, and so before I knew I was part of this city, felt at home, hence resisted buying a map. I could not admit I needed one, it took even longer before I bought a little guide book and skipped through the biography of the Most Serene Republic to discover that I had already read her history while drawing the stones, the carved lintels, capitols, columns and arches, while criscrossing Venice day after day, just following my nose, walking with eyes wide open, sketchbook at the ready.

I said walking: one cannot afford to trudge , for too much escapes the eye unless the head is kept mobile on its admirably designed swivel bracket: it has to shift constantly from marble pavement to wisps of cloud over the Piazzetta, from wisps of girls to formidable matrons, from deep black water to pillared facades, from tourists to gondolas, to all those stone tablets, set overhead in old walls: noble family crests, cherubs, singing, angels winging, saints blessing, fabled animals, imaginary monsters. There must be a thousand winged lions on these tablets: they growl, smile, weep dejectedly, and numberless Madonnas who nurse their Babes, lift them for all to see, rock them, lifeless, on their knees in Pietas. One of these Holy Virgins - she spans the Calle del Paradiso - spreads the cloak of her mercy over generations of us, ephemerals, who pass underneath.

"No architect should be allowed to practice his trade," says Professor Garrett Hardin of Santa Barbara, "until he has lived a year in Venice and knows what a city is, built to human scale." Not only is Venice built to human scale, it is the last surviving human city, the last habitat remaining on our planet still fully human in its patterns of hubris and humility, of life. Constantly astonished is one here by what should not be astonishing at all, except to us, so used, so conditioned to accept the machine's priority over all living flesh, to heed stop/go traffic lights, being demoted to the rank of pedestrian, that is: shorn of human rights until once again behind the wheel. Here, at last, the category pedestrian does not apply, for everyone still walks, or at most stands, once in a while compressed between fellow bipeds on the quavering deck of a vaporetto.

Venice is an immense and living indoor and outdoor studio. I can sit down to draw in peace on any bench, any stoop or folding stool, on any Campo - as the squares are called here - in the middle of any street, whether narrow Calle or wider Salizada or dead-end Corte. No one interrupts me or assaults me, no mugger robs me.

Submerged in this Venetian life, my seeing/drawing of Venice is both more and less than a declaration of love for the Serenissima, who has been loved by so many. Most of her lovers were writers. Goethe, Byron, Shelley, Ruskin shared in her favors, and batallions of lesser men of letters - of word - have reported all about her irresistible charms, her flawed and glorious past, so that not a shred of information needs to be added, and should any "information" sneak into what follows, it might be considered as an adhesive to tie a few drawings together. both as witness and incentive to pure experience, an eye in love.

I return to Venice only when the technicolor prettiness of summer has faded, the city has shed her garish summer dress. Venice only gives herself unreservedly on the sun-flecked foggy days of Fall and early Spring, and in the dead of winter, with hoarfrost on the tangled little wildernesses behind cracked garden walls. It is not comfortable to draw her then, with running nose and icecold fingers, but the light, a translucent grisaille enlivened with a moist pale gold sun, weaves the city and its shifting patterns of past and present in a warp and woof of scintillation and dimness in which the eye becomes fully identified with the water, the flights of pearlgrey pigeons, the timeless choreography of lovers. Old men in overcoats sit on benches, breathing in the sea air saturated with pollutants from the smoke stacks of Mestre and Marghera across the bay; discrete pollutants, just strong enough to gnaw away the noses and nipples of bronze and marble goddesses.

How still the city is in this greyness, where starlings can still be heard chirping, canaries mix their bel canto with the voices of children and cooing mammas. Far away, men are argueing in a twitter not noisier, yet not less noisy than a tree full of sparrows: choruses of lifesounds they are, in a timeless silence only made audible by the deep throated throb of vaporettos.

•

San Giacomo dall'Orio on its tree-shade campo has none of the grandeur of the San Marco. It is of unaffected inwardness, untouched by the rising and falling of history's ebb and flow, as if it were standing somewhere on a mountain top, unreachable even by the high tides of tourism. It is not included in the "musts." Dark and taciturn, its entrances hard to find, no one corrupted it, made sanctuary into museum, no polyglot guides offer platitudes.

San Giacomo simply is not this, not that. It is. It still echoes sacred messages in a code that is lost, whispers meanings to be pondered, not articulated, wordless prayer. Its frescoes are homey, its polychromed Madonna rustically maternal. Could its secret be condensed in the twelfth-century Crucifix that hangs in a side chapel against the bare brick wall? Is it a crucifixion, or a resurrection, or both at once, this Christ of wood, without cross, who hangs there, this Christ who smiles with a smile from The Other Shore?

It is not the Buddha's smile of supernal wisdom, detached compassion. Yet it has all the wisdom and all the Compassion, but distilled through all the joys of body and spirit, all exaltation and all the terror, all the pain that flesh can endure. It participates in all the greatness and all the bottomlessly cruel, blind absurdities of our human species, which never sees what it looks at, hence never knows what it does, what it perpetrates. It is as if this fully Human Christ cries his "It is finished," and rising to Heaven, smiling, whispers: "It is not, oh no, it is not finished, it is not finished..."

The Christ of San Giacomo, the Nicopeia Madonna of San Marco: to this agnostic, this not-knower, are the harmonious poles, male and female, of this still human city, this Serenissima.

Epilogue: The Cosmic Fish

I must have been about twelve when I came to add a symbol all my own to the official iconography. In the local newspaper I saw the photograph of an almost two-thousand-year-old stone carving of a fish. It had just been unearthed in Rome's catacombs. According to the caption, the fish—ichtos in Greek—was the oldest symbol of Christ.

It was unavoidable in a town as Catholic as ours that I caught some talk about the Church as the "Mystical Body of Christ." I had no idea what that might mean, but it kept resonating in me as an organ chord until "Mystical Body" and the ancient Fish fused into a single image, that of a gigantic Fish. Each one of its numberless scales carried a human face, white, brown, black, yellow. All of humanity was peering at you from the Fish's scales.

On evening walks my imagination let the Great Fish take off from a huddle of old houses around the Basilica, built a thousand years ago on the ruins of a Roman Jupiter temple. I saw the Fish rise into the night sky, saw it cross the river Meuse to sail through the interstellar spaces in the direction of the constellation Orion.

The image never faded. Many years later when I read in Kegon Buddhist writings about the "radical interdependence of all phenomena in the Universe," I met my Cosmic Fish in Chinese Buddhist garb. It had become transcultural, transreligious, embodiment and symbol of that radical interdependence—to the point of mutual interpenetration—of all living things on earth and in the cosmos, a seventh-century preview of what we now give names like "deep ecology": the Oneness of the Many, the Manyness of the one.

It may well have been this Cosmic Fish that kept me from ever joining any church, sect, even Zen center, any circumscribed in-group. It made me into the loner whose single allegiance seems to be transreligious, to the All-Encompassing Fish, throughout a long life that has almost flashed by. Through the years I have drawn the Cosmic Fish, painted it, engraved it, sculpted it in stone, in wood and steel, fired it on stained glass. Still, I never caught the Fish; it caught me.

Acknowledgements

If I were to list all those who inspired and encouraged me through my ninety-four years on this planet, it would require a separate volume! It would have to include each one the musicians of my home town, who touched me—I was perhaps twelve—playing works like Verdi's "Agnus Dei" and Faure's "In Paradiso" as the most heart-rendering outcries of the human spirit.

Then, there were the painters and those few poets and the deaf-mute sculptor Eyck. These artists I idolized. They confirmed that all I really loved and honored was subsumed under the heading "art" and all that repelled and even frightened me, under that of "business," of buying and selling, even the doctoring, to which I seemed inescapably predestined.

As a medical student, I discovered Rilke and those wondrous ancient Chinese poets Du Fu and Li Po, the Upanishads, Chuang Tzu, Zen thanks to Daisetz Teitaro Suzuki, Meister Eckhart and of course Johann Sebastian Bach, the Vox Humana of the Divine. I felt ever inspired by the 17th century Dutch draftsmen, above all by the incomparable Rembrandt's Holland landscapes.

An ever worsening deafness and a deterioration of eye-sight seem to make me hear and see *That Which Matters,* not less, but more clearly.

Warm thanks go out to those companions on the Way, to David Appelbaum, publisher/editor of this book, to Martin Moskof, its designer, to my son Lucas, to Frances Louise Jennick, indefatigable editorial assistant, and to Claske without whom all this and life itself IS unthinkable.

◆

Typesetting by Graphic Communications & Product Design, Inc
Set in ITC Garamond and Garamond italic.
Type design by the great French designer Claude Garamond in c.1540.
Written and drawn by Frederick Franck
Published and edited by David Appelbaum
Photography by John Stage • Design by Martin Moskof
Editorial assistance by Claske Berndes Franck and Frances Louise Jennick
Paperback first edition of 1500 copies • Printed by McNaughton-Gunn, USA